To Ric

the best is yet to come

Kenzell Moss

Kenzell Evans
BREAKING THE SILENCE

authorHOUSE®

AuthorHouse™
1663 Liberty Drive
Bloomington, IN 47403
www.authorhouse.com
Phone: 1-800-839-8640

Published by AuthorHouse   11/30/2012

ISBN: 978-1-4772-5638-1 (sc)
ISBN: 978-1-4772-5637-4 (hc)
ISBN: 978-1-4772-5636-7 (e)

Library of Congress Control Number: 2012914399

I am dedicating this book to my wife, my son and his family, my daughter, and my nephews, and nieces. To the new generation that will face the realities of life with open-mindedness, sincerity, frankness, and love for themselves and others.

This is a true story, some names have been changed.

THE BACKBONE

The North Carolina town of Hamlet, just six miles south of Rockingham, had three traffic lights in the center of town. It was segregated and had a population of about 4,000. There were a lot of black churches and three schools for the blacks. There were more schools for the whites and they were bus to and from school. The blacks had to walk. There were more whites than blacks, and the whites owned everything.

A fairly typical southern country town, it sits on mostly flat land, with a few hills here and there, as well as lakes, lots of pine trees, and dirt roads. Outside of town were the farms, with mostly tobacco and cotton fields.

The stores were downtown on Hamlet Ave. and Main Street. On Hamlet Ave. were a barber shop, a beauty parlor, a pool hall for whites, a cafe, a furniture store, a general store, and a clothing store. Down on Main Street was a little hotel, a small movie theater, and a hardware store. Across the street were a five and dime store, and a shoe store to name a few. Further up was the police station, the fire station, and a gas station. The icehouse, the bus station, and the fish house were around the corner.

Merchants pulled up in either a horse and buggy or a horse and wagon to do their shopping, getting what supplies they needed. There were a few cars around too.

Across the railroad tracks was a pool hall for blacks, and up from that was the train station. The main feature that distinguished Hamlet from many other small southern towns was that it was the largest train depot in the area, a very busy one too, and the only one for miles around. It was the hub, with trains running in all four directions. When a train stopped there, whites would use the front entrance, blacks the rear. In fact, they were not allowed to enter the front of any establishment. Trains often remained there for a good while, for cars to be added or disconnected, repairs to be made, and supplies to be replenished.

The people of Hamlet and the surrounding area kept busy. Of course, the whites always got the best jobs.

Fort Bragg was about 65 miles from Hamlet. The soldiers stationed there spent a lot of time in Hamlet, as did those in transit to or from Fort Bragg. All during World War II it was an exciting place for the troops, a place where they could go and have a good time, and that kept business booming. The soldiers loved it, and the townspeople welcomed them.

Hamlet had become a party town. In the '40s and '50s it was the place to be. There were bars and clubs everywhere, with lots of drinking and dancing going on. You could get just about anything you wanted. There were lots of bootleggers who dealt in home brew or corn liquor. They would go to the train depot, patiently wait around for a train to come in, and then approach the folks who were alighting from it and try to make a sale.

I was raised by my grandparents, Emma and Bruce Evans. I grew up believing they were my parents, and nobody ever told me otherwise. I called them Mama and Papa. My name is Kenzell. I was born on Easter Sunday and they called me Barney.

My "parents" supported me and gave me lots of love. I was their youngest child, and much younger than the others, so they gave me more than my share of their attention.

Mama was a brown-skinned woman with a medium build, an oval-shaped face, thick eyebrows that nearly met, and rich hair. She was about 5'6" in height and weighed about 185 pounds. She was rather good looking and had class. She was neat and carried herself with grace and style. She wanted and loved nice things. One of her hobbies was stamp collecting. She had several books full of stamps. She was very particular about what she wore and wouldn't consider going out in public looking disheveled. She loved getting her hair done, and dressing up for church. She attended Second Baptist New Hope and was there every Sunday and always took me with her.

Papa worked for the Seaboard Railroad at the depot. He had light brown skin, a narrow-shaped face, and wavy hair. He was a handsome man, one who dressed nicely. His clothes were always pressed. He was about 5'7", had a slim frame, and weighed about 155 pounds. He was an easy-go-lucky guy, not having much to say except when he was away from the house.

There were eight of us, four girls, Pam, Nora, Lisa, and Peaches; and four boys, Bob, Steve, Roger, and me, none of whom was over 5'7". By the time I was seven, all but Peaches, Roger, and me had moved away, Bob, my oldest brother, left before I was born and joined the service. My oldest sister, Pam, was married and lived nearby with her husband Billy and their six children. Steve also lived nearby, with his wife Donna and their newborn son. Nora lived in Washington, D.C. with her husband Joe and their five children. Lisa moved to Charlotte, N.C., where she lived with her husband Frank and their three children.

We lived in the southern part of Hamlet, right at the edge of town, in a big wooden house. It had three bedrooms, a living room, an eat-in kitchen, and another room where Mama kept two freezer chests: one for ice cream, cakes, and pies, and one for meats, chicken, and fish. In that room there were also shelves stacked with food that she had jarred.

The house had front and back porches and an outhouse. We had a large pecan tree, several plum trees, an apple tree, and grapevines. We had two horses, a mule, a few cows, some hogs, lots of chickens, about three or four hound dogs, and Papa's cats.

During cotton-picking season, everybody who needed money picked cotton: most were blacks, young and old. I was too young to pull tobacco or pick cotton. Peaches and Roger would get up early in the morning and stand on the other side of the road with some other people, waiting for the white man to come with the bus that would pick them up and then drop them off late at night.

That was how some made their living. The young had to work as long as it took to get enough money to buy their school clothes. As a result, some of them didn't start school on time. Many of them didn't like that, but they had no choice.

Mama was the backbone of the family. She kept everything and everybody together and raised us to be that way. She was a giving and caring woman. She was strong and hard working.

Mama was a true farmer who knew how to live off the land. She grew her own vegetables on our 45-acre plot. All of us worked in the field and around the house.

She killed two hogs and a cow every year and made sure there was enough food to go around, not only for all her kids but also for relatives and close friends. She loved to eat. Her two favorites were pig's feet, and coconut cake with butter pecan ice cream.

Steve worked at the Butter Cup, an ice cream plant. He always brought ice cream to the house for Mama and kept her freezer filled with different flavors, all in five-gallon containers.

On one occasion she became ill, and Dr. Brown was called. He was a short, fat man who made house calls.

"Mrs. Evans, you know you have high blood pressure. Your pressure is very high right now, so I'm going to change your medication and you'll need to stay away from the pork and the salt shaker."

She just looked at him. Later that week, Mama was up on her feet again and eating everything as before.

When she got up in the morning she would come into my room and say,

"Barney, wake up, its time to get up."

In fact, she woke everybody up.

One of my chores was to gather eggs from the hen house every morning. Mama cooked breakfast and prepared lunch for everybody. On school days she'd give me some fruit and at least three biscuit sandwiches for my lunch. She'd pack a mix of biscuits from her repertoire: ham, mayonnaise and jelly, bacon, peanut butter and jelly, sausage and egg.

After seeing us off to school, she'd wash clothes and then go work in the field. When she came back to the house, she would jar up food and then go back outside and kill two or three chickens. She would pick and clean the chickens, cut them up, and start making dinner on her old steel stove. She was a mighty good cook and could prepare anything on that stove.

Mama believed in cleaning up. Before day's end she would go out and rake the yard. There was no grass, just a dirt yard. When she raked the dirt, there would be dust everywhere.

Constantly pushing me hard to do well in school, Mama helped me with my homework. She made me put my books under my pillow when I went to bed at night, and she quizzed me the next morning to make sure I remembered what I had studied. She was very strict with me when it came to school.

"You're very good in math and spelling. Make something out of your life, and try to be somebody. If you want something in life, work for it, and keep striving until you get it. Be strong. I love you. You're my baby."

One day in the middle of the second week of school, a boy in my classroom approached me.

"Do you want to sell one of your sandwiches? I'll give you a nickel for it."

"I'll sell you a sandwich."

He told a few other boys that I was selling sandwiches. I didn't mind. I figured that the more money I earned, the more candy and cookies I could buy at the store near the house. I began to look forward to selling sandwiches every day.

I tried to think of ways to get Mama to make me more sandwiches, and I would make some myself when she wasn't looking. It was near the end of the week when the boys suddenly stopped buying my sandwiches. I went to them and tried to find out why. They said they had no more money. One boy bought for a few more days, and then he stopped too.

One day Mama was summoned to the school. I had gotten into a fight with one of the boys because he had stopped buying my sandwiches. I told Mama that he had been teasing me about my hair and that he kept saying I had bees in my head.

"There's nothing wrong with your hair. It's rich, like mine. You just have to grease it and keep it brushed. I keep telling you that. If they hit you, you hit them back. And remember: Sticks and stones can break your bones, but words can never hurt you."

Papa didn't care to work in the field. When he wasn't at work at the train depot, he spent his time hunting and fishing or would go visit some of his friends. On those occasions Mama would say,

"Take Barney with you."

He and I would go see his co-workers and then his girlfriends. Before visiting the latter, he would say,

"Keep your mouth shut or I won't take you anywhere else with me."

I assured him that my lips were sealed.

He would buy me anything I wanted. Then before heading for home, we'd stop at the fish house.

He said, "Charlie, give me a pound of those fish heads."

"They're fresh, Bruce," said the proprietor.

Then Papa turned to me and said.

"This is for dinner."

"I'm not eating that mess."

He just chuckled.

When we got home he threw the bag of fish heads on the table and said, "I stopped and got some dinner."

Mama replied, "You mean you got your cats some dinner. We don't eat fish heads here, unless you want them for yourself."

The following morning, when I went to get the eggs, I saw that Mama had put the fish heads out for the cats. They were fighting over them. When I went back inside, I told Mama what I had seen.

"Mama, the cats are fighting over the fish heads."

"That's to be expected. They hadn't eaten in a few days. Your daddy said they're in training, so what you see is what you get. Those are his cats. I'm surprised they haven't killed one of his dogs."

"They're almost as big as the dogs are now."

"I know."

Papa wasn't a big drinker, but he had friends who were, so he'd make home brew and corn whiskey just for them. When it was ready he'd invite them over after work, usually on weekends. They would sit under the shade tree and drink. If Pam and Lisa were home, Papa's friends would sneak around the house when he wasn't looking and talk to them.

Sometimes he invited his drinking buddies to come over for dinner and tried to fill them up on watermelon. By the time dinner was ready they would be full. He thought he had them right where he wanted them, so he could get their money. They didn't seem to care as long as they had a chance to see his daughters.

Papa came home one day and broke the latest news to Mama.

"I heard that Dr. Brown passed away."

"What happened?"

"I'm not sure. I heard he had health problems and that he died of a heart attack. He also had sugar diabetes and high blood pressure. Somebody mentioned a stroke too."

"And he was giving other people advice. He should have saved some of that for himself."

"Barney, come and help me hitch the horse up to the wagon so we can go into town to get supplies."

"Cut his hair before y'all leave."

"I was just about to do that."

Papa had a pair of dull hand clippers that he used to cut my hair, leaving patches of hair all over my head, but I didn't care as long as I got to go along. When he took me into town with him I always knew he would buy me something.

At one time Papa had a '38 Model-T Ford, the kind you cranked up in the front to get it started. He eventually got rid of it, but I wished he had kept it. He often said,

"I was tired of spending money on that damned thing, but I kept putting off getting rid of it. I just didn't want to walk to work."

We lived within easy walking distance of the train station, only half a mile or so.

Mama loved to travel, and since Papa worked for the railroad, she could ride the train free of charge. When she did, she took me with her. She always told people, "That's my baby. He's smart and does well in school. He's going to make something of himself."

Once or twice a year, she and I traveled by train to visit Lisa and Nora as well as Mama's brothers and some other relatives who lived in Petersburg, VA. and Baltimore, MD. She always took food for them, and always gave them a heads up by sending a card to let them know which day we would arrive. She never said how long we'd be staying.

Every time we went to Nora's place I immediately noticed the bugs. They were everywhere. I wasn't used to seeing that, and it startled me. It didn't seem to bother anyone of Nora's kids. One time I asked Mama about the bugs.

"Mama, what are those?"

"Be quiet."

A few hours after we arrived, Mama would say something to the effect that we couldn't stay long, claiming she had a lot of work to do when we got back home. It wasn't that she had anything in particular to do. She just didn't want to impose on Nora. Besides, there was nowhere for us to sleep at Nora's place, and there was no food in the house other than what Mama had brought along — for them and brought along for us.

"You haven't yet been here for six hours and you're ready to leave?"

"I know, but we've stayed longer than I had planned. You're not the only one I came to see."

"You said that the last time you were here."

"I'll stay longer next time, but I have to get back today."

On our way home Mama answered the question I had asked about the bugs.

"Those bugs are called roaches. I don't like them either, and I sure couldn't eat or sleep there with those bugs crawling around. That's why I packed enough food for you and me."

"I didn't like it there."

"Don't worry, baby, I wasn't about to stay there for long."

Mama died in 1957. I was only eight years old. I couldn't believe it. I was speechless. This was an extremely sad time for me. The tears constantly ran down my face. I wanted my Mama. I couldn't believe she was gone.

Roger said, "Now that Mama's gone, what are we going to do?"

Roger and I were the only two still living at home at that time. Peaches had gotten married and had two kids. She was living overseas with her husband John, who was in the service.

Some people came to the house to take Mama's body away. When they returned, her body was in a casket, which they placed in the living room. It had a smell that I'll never forget. She lay there with her eyes closed as if she were asleep.

During the next few days everybody in the family came home, including Peaches. They had prepared lots of food. Other relatives and some friends came by later and also brought food.

On the evening before the burial, even more people came in to see her. They were all sitting around, eating, drinking, and talking. It seemed as though nobody was leaving, perhaps because Papa had pulled out his home brew and corn whiskey. Peaches said,

"Barney, go into your room and go to bed."

I did, but I was unable to sleep. I felt alone. I lay there crying and thinking about my Mama, trying to understand why she was gone.

She died of cancer but had never told anyone she was sick. I hadn't suspected that there was anything wrong with her, for she was always busy doing something and never complained about a thing.

After everybody had left the house that night it was very quiet. The next morning we went out into the woods, where they buried her. Nothing was ever the same after that.

Peaches and her family left right after the funeral. The others left shortly thereafter, including Roger. He had been dating a girl from Durham. She had come to the funeral, and he went back with her. I was the only one who stayed home with Papa.

Shortly after Mama's death, Papa had a stroke that affected his speech and caused paralysis on the right side of his body. There was talk about me going to Washington to live with Nora, because of Papa's inability to take care of me.

"You have to go live with Nora now. Lisa got in touch with her, and she'll be coming to get you. I'm not able to take care of you. As you can see, I have to get somebody to take care of me."

"I don't want to go. I want to stay here. Roger and I will be all right. I can stay with Pam."

"I don't think Roger's coming back, and Pam has no room for you and no time to care for you. Don't worry. You'll be okay. Get your education, and make me proud of you. And keep a smile on your face. You know Mama would like that."

I cried and cried, and did everything I could think of to persuade Papa to let me stay there, but to no avail. It had already been decided where I was going.

UNWELCOME

Nora came home and took me back with her. She lived in an upstairs one-bedroom apartment in a four-unit apartment building.

Jack was her oldest child. He was one year older than me. His full name was Jack Wells. He was light skinned, had curly hair and a narrow face, was short (about 4'2"), and weighed about 70 pounds. I think I had it over him by a few inches and several pounds. All Jack ever wanted to do was play. He was never concerned about what the others wanted to do, and he exhibited a lack of responsibility.

Then there was Sean, Sean Wells, who was two years younger than me. Like Jack, he was light skinned, had curly hair and a narrow face, and was short. He was quiet and passive and did everything Jack tell him to do.

Patrice was the oldest girl. Four years younger than me, she had light skin, long wavy hair, large eyes, and a pretty smile. She was very attractive, though short, and she talked very fast. She was presumptuous. Give her an inch, and she would take a mile — and then brag about it.

Paula, who was five years younger than me, was light skinned and short and had wavy hair. She too was attractive. Paula had a habit of sticking her nose into things that were none of her business. She was selfish and wanted attention—and, like Jack, she had no sense of responsibility.

Nora's youngest child was Kim. She was seven years younger than me. She was dark skinned, had rich kinky hair, and was rather cute, but they called her Buckwheat and I never understand why.

I didn't like being there. All I saw was buildings, concrete, roaches, and kids running and playing in the streets. I wanted to go back home, to what I was used to and the place where I had lived with my family.

I was still mourning the loss of Mama, but nobody seemed to care.

At home, everybody had cared and Mama had always been there. Here, nobody cared and Nora was always gone.

I had gone without eating for the first two days I was there, though I did drink water. I felt uncomfortable about eating the food — it didn't look safe with the roaches crawling over it — but I knew I had to eat something or I would get too weak to function. When I finally did eat, it was apple butter and peanut butter sandwiches. I was more leery than picky.

For the first week or so I didn't sleep very well. I was concerned about the roaches. I sat on the floor with my back against the wall and eventually fell asleep.

One day I mentioned to Nora that I wanted to go back home. She said, "This is your home now. I'm your mother, and these are your brothers and sisters."

This was the first time I had ever heard this. I thought to myself, she's not my mother?

She was an older sister of mine. Mama had never hinted anything to me — or anyone else, as far as I knew.

"You're not my mother, and they're not my brothers and sisters. I want to go home."

"I am your mother and they are your brothers and sisters."

"No you're not."

This conversation was repeated a number of times over the next several weeks. I tried to adjust, but I wasn't accepted by Nora and her family. They were always calling me names. This was so different from life back home in Hamlet.

I took to being quiet, keeping mostly to myself, and going with the flow. I didn't like it at Nora's and didn't want to be there. My new environment was turning my life upside down.

What little furniture Nora had was no good. A worn-out, broke down bed with the springs sticking out, two dressers with three drawers missing, a sofa bed that had fabric worn down to the wood on both arms, and a dirty mattress on the floor. She had a yellow kitchen table with silver legs, and two broken matching chairs.

They had no drinking glasses. They drank out of peanut butter, mayonnaise and jelly jars.

One morning, I stood in the kitchen and watched them eating breakfast. Two of them were sitting on the table with their legs folded, and they had plastic bowls in front of them. Also on the table was a mayonnaise jar filled with water, a box of white powder, and a large bag of

Wheat Puffs cereal. They mixed the water and powder together to make milk for their cereal.

They stuffed down the food as if they hadn't eaten in weeks. The roaches were everywhere, crawling around looking for something to eat. They just smacked them with their hands or stepped on them with their bare feet and then continued eating.

In the refrigerator there was a box of cheese, a jar of apple butter, powdered eggs, a jar of peanut butter, and some kind of canned meat. I found out later that this was called welfare food.

Whenever there was bread in the apartment, they would tear open the wrapper somewhere in the middle and start eating.

I had never seen anything like it before. There was never enough food to go around, and Nora hadn't done any cooking since I arrived. At home there had always been plenty of food to eat. Even if you didn't want it, it was there.

Patrice said, "We don't want you eating up our food, Black Sambo."

Sean added, "We don't want you here anyway. You need to go back to the country, Country Boy."

Then Jack chimed in.

"You had to come and stay with us, didn't you? We were doing just fine until you came here."

"I don't want to be here either."

I hadn't yet seen or met Nora's husband. He had never been around when Mama and I visited, nor do I remember Mama's ever asking Nora about him. Nora wasn't working, but she was still gone most of the time. When she was there she played cards by herself, and at times showed her kids how to play various card games. What she most loved to do was play cards and playing numbers while chewing on Doublemint gum. She would sit and play cards for hours at a time.

The kids did whatever they wanted, and Nora said nothing to them. I just sat around and watched them. They didn't know their ABCs, couldn't count to 100, and couldn't spell. I couldn't believe the things I was seeing and hearing from them. I thought something was wrong with them, but I kept my thoughts to myself.

The neighborhood kids were always beating them up and taking their toys from them. They would come into the house crying instead of staying outside and fighting back. I would say to them,

"Go hit them back, and get your toys."

But they would just stand there, looking at me and crying. I didn't understand that. They could tease me, but they wouldn't fight back when others did them wrong. I had been raised to fight back: *If somebody hits you, you hit them back.*

One day Paula came in crying, and I went outside and beat up the boy who had pushed her to the ground. He was older than she was. When we came back into the house I gave her some advice.

"You should have hit him back."

"He's bigger and older than me."

"So what, you still should have hit him back."

"He's older than me too."

"You still should have hit him back."

She just looked at me as if I was supposed to protect her because I was older.

From that day on, I protected them. Every time they had a problem or got into trouble, they called me. I was playing the role of big brother.

Whenever they wanted something, they called me Barney or Kenzell. Otherwise, they called me Black Sambo or Black Country Boy, or just ignored me altogether. I soon got used to the name-calling.

I didn't mind helping them. It made me feel wanted, and not realizing what I had gotten myself into, I thought it was the right thing to do, something that would bring us closer together.

There was another bully in the neighborhood, a boy that picked on Sean a lot. Knowing that I was there, he said to Sean, "You think you're safe now because your big brother is here, but he won't be around all the time. I'll get you."

One day Nora again brought up the subject of my relationship to her.

"You can call me Mama, like they do."

"You're not my mother."

"I am your mother."

I didn't say anything more. I just looked at her, thinking about the names Jack and the rest of them had been calling me and how I was being treated. Nora knew they had been saying those things, but she never corrected them.

Not long after I arrived at Nora's place, we moved. We went to stay with a woman named Ms. Walker. She was a nice person. They called her Big Mama. She lived in a white, three-bedroom duplex that sat right at the edge of the street. Ms. Walker had two daughters, Rita and May. Rita had four kids, two boys and two girls: Billy, Wade, Laura, and Sarah. May had three girls: Jan, Sheila, and Wendy.

Counting Nora and her six kids, there were seventeen people living in that house. We stayed there for about ten months and then moved into a two-bedroom apartment building.

It wasn't until after that move that I met Joe, Joe Wells, Nora's husband. He was a light-skinned man, handsome, with a medium but muscular build. Jack looked just like him. Joe had a full head of black wavy hair, was about 5'7" in height, weighed about 180 pounds, and wore glasses.

Joe lived with us now, and he drove a dump truck for a living. At first he was there all the time. Then he started hanging out with his friends, drinking, partying, and such. When he was home, all he did was watch cartoons, drink liquor, and tell Nora what to do.

THEY ALL LAUGHED

When I was about ten or eleven years old, my life began to change, I felt alone, more so than ever before. I enjoyed school and wanted to do well, but my heart was no longer in it. I wasn't happy. I wanted to go back home to North Carolina. Here nobody really cared about me or what I was doing. At Nora's I felt left out, and not like a part of her family. I had tried so hard to belong, but the harder I tried, the more they pushed me away.

As time went on I began to realize how different I was from the rest. They never saw eye to eye with me on anything. Also, all of them had the same last name, Wells, but my last name was Evans. And all of them were light skinned—all, that is, but Kim and me. Other than having the same mother, I had nothing in common with them.

The only times I meant anything to them were the times when they wanted me to protect them.

There was very little communication between us. We didn't play together, nor did we do anything together like a normal family. In fact, we didn't do anything together at all. Joe and Nora did their thing, their kids had their friends, and I had mine. There was no love or togetherness at all. In fact, the word *love* was never used.

Though my relationship with them had never been very good, having Joe around was even worse. One day he said, "Damn! You have so many bees in your head that it looks like a cornfield. You do look like Black Sambo."

They all laughed.

"Don't you forget that you came to live with us, so don't be trying to tell my kids what to do."

"I'm not telling them what to do."

"You'd better not be."

At that moment he let me know where we stood. They laughed and started teasing me more—and repeating everything he and Nora said, and they never corrected them.

I eventually figured out that Nora wasn't playing cards just for enjoyment. She was a gambler. She had friends who played cards too, and they would talk for hours about a game: how much money they had won or lost, and where the next one would be held.

She hosted game sessions at our place, at times staying up all night playing cards and continuing until noon the next day. Playing numbers games was another of her passions. If it wasn't cards, it was numbers. She was obsessed with both.

Nora had gotten a job at a place called Miss Ray's Diner. When it was time for a new school year to begin, Nora got Jack and Sean each at least three sets of clothes, and the girls got three or four dresses. They got coats and shoes as usual.

She said to me, "I got you two shirts and a pair of pants. I ran out of money. I'll get the rest of your things when I get paid."

They always laughed and teased me about what they got and what I didn't get. I acted as if it didn't bother me, but it did.

Nora treated me as if I was beneath them, and they acted like it too. I started drifting away, mentally speaking, and losing interest in everything, especially school, which I had always loved before. It wasn't a matter of not being able to do the work. I didn't have decent clothes to wear.

I had been wearing the same clothes day after day. When I washed them out they weren't always completely dry by morning, so I had to wear them to school partially wet, which was especially unpleasant on cold days.

The few acquaintances I had made probably had no inkling of how I was living. I did all I could to prevent them from knowing. If they noticed anything, they kept it to themselves.

At times when I was alone, I cried for my Mama.

"Mama, what's going on? Why am I being treated the way I am? I miss you. I wish you were here."

Sometimes I would just sit and think about cousins of mine back home: Wondering what they were doing and wish I was there with them. But I never let anybody see me in this mood, for I had always been told to be strong.

My classmates had been joking and teasing me about the holes in my shoes, and the rubber bands around my shoes, and my dirty cloths. My feet stank so bad that they kept their distance from me.

I had put rubber bands around the toe area of my shoes to stop the flapping when I walk. When the soles got to bad, I cut them off and put cardboard in the shoes to cover the holes. On rainy days I carried extra cardboard in my pockets, because by the time I got to school my feet would be cold and wet. I would go straight to the bathroom and put dry cardboard in my shoes.

When Christmas and Easter came around I wasn't at all excited. I just knew I would be treated the same as usual — and that's exactly what happened. Nora gave me her standard excuse: "I ran out of money. I'll get your things later."

I was still wearing those same clothes, and my shoes now had big holes in them.

"My shoes have holes in them, and I need a coat."

"I'll get you a coat."

I didn't say a thing. I just looked at her, and they all laughed at me.

I got tired of the embarrassment and no longer wanted to be seen looking the way I did, so I started skipping school. The counselor wanted to know why I was absent so often.

A letter from the school arrived one day, stating that I had been expelled and wouldn't be permitted to return without my parents. I threw it in the trash. I had made up my mind I wasn't going back until Nora bought me some new clothes, a coat, and shoes.

Nora was there when the next letter arrived.

"Why haven't you been going to school? Why are you skipping school?"

"I don't have anything to wear. I'm tired of going to school looking like this. I'm tired of it."

"Tired of what? Jack and Sean go to school every day."

"Jack and Sean have clothes, shoes, and a coat to wear. It's not the same. It's cold outside. Look at me! Look at my shoes! I'm not going to school looking like this anymore."

The tears were flowing from my eyes and running down my face.

"You want me to buy you expensive clothes and shoes?"

"I never said anything about expensive clothes. I don't know where you got that from."

"I'm going to get you some clothes, a pair of shoes, and a coat when I get paid, and I'm going to get you back in school."

I never found out what she told the counselor, but I was allowed back in school.

"When you get home, wash those clothes you have on, tonight. They're dirty, and they stink."

"What do you expect? These are the only clothes I have. I'm not wearing this to school anymore."

"I'm going to buy you new clothes."

I didn't say anything more and I didn't know what to do. I wanted to believe her, but I couldn't. She'd made that same promise so many times before, and it had always proved to be empty.

I did wash out my clothes, and I didn't go back to school. I roamed the streets instead. After a week of that I asked Nora, "When are you going to get me some shoes to wear and what happened to the clothes you said you were going to get me?"

She started yelling!

"Boy, I don't have any money. You should be thankful you have a roof over your head. You're never going to amount to shit anyway. Get out of my face."

I continued skipping school.

When she finally got me some shoes, my feet were full of cuts and blisters and they were sore. She didn't say where she had gotten the shoes, but they weren't new. The nails in the heels were sticking me in the feet.

"These shoes are too big, causing my feet to slide backward and forward. My feet are already sore, and the nails from the heels are sticking me in the feet."

"Why do you have to be so difficult? You should be thankful you have some shoes."

I wanted to say something, but I didn't. I decided it would be better to deal with the pain than to hear her mouthing off to me.

Then she walked over to me and said, "I'll buy you a pair of shoes on payday."

When payday came around she bought me a pair of tennis shoes for sixty-nine cents. They were made of plastic. She must have known that they wouldn't last long. They lasted about an hour, and then the bottoms fell out.

She couldn't help but hear the laughing and teasing that was going on in the house about my shoes. Instead of putting a stop to it, she yelled at me!

"I know you couldn't have already torn up those shoes I just bought you. Why are you so hard on shoes?"

"These things are plastic. What do you expect?"

"Jack and Sean's shoes last. They aren't hard on their shoes."

"You got them U.S. Keds."

"Just shut up! You just want some expensive shoes. I'm not buying you any. I'm not going to be spending my money on shoes for you to tear up. You can go barefoot for all I care."

I thought of a way to fix the shoes with the nails sticking me in the heels: I got a brick and bent the nails as best I could. Then I put cardboard over that area and stuffed newspaper in the toe area.

One evening I was outside playing, and when I came in to eat there was no food left. Joe scolded me.

"You should have been in here when everybody else was eating. Now wash the dishes."

"It's not my week to wash the dishes. It's Jack's week. When they're not in here, you make sure that they eat. Paula wasn't in here yesterday, and you made sure that she had something to eat."

"I don't care whose week it is."

Nora came into the kitchen and said, "Just shut up. You knew I was cooking. You should have been in here. So just shut up and wash those dishes! And when you finish, go into the other room."

I was tired of this place and tired of them. Nora always went along with Joe, right or wrong. No matter what he said, she agreed.

One evening, Sean and Patrice were teasing me because they had eaten all the food. They had left none for me. Out of anger, I made an attempt to hit them.

Joe immediately jumped up!

"Don't put your damned hands on *my* kids. I don't care *what* they've done."

They were laughing, sticking their tongues out at me, calling me names, and making faces, but Joe did nothing to stop them. That made me feel as if he was giving them permission to say and do anything to me that they wanted. That took a lot out of me, but when he wasn't around I took my revenge. It also reminded me of something my mama had always said: *Sticks and stones can break your bones, but words can never hurt you.*

Whenever something at our place was missing or broken, Nora automatically accused me of doing it — and punished me whether I had done it or not.

"Barney is the one who did it. He's always into something."

"I don't know what you're talking about. I wasn't here when it happened."

"No one did it but you. I can tell when you're lying."

The others could do no wrong. They were the perfect kids, the golden kids, in Nora and Joe's eyes, and Nora made no secret of it if every asked. "They're doing just fine. I have no problems with them. They're good kids. Kenzell is the only one we have problems with. His head is hard. He doesn't want to go to school, and he pretends to be a grownup, but he doesn't have a pot to piss in or a window to throw it out of."

Nothing positive was ever said about me. And Nora always found a way to justify her actions toward me.

Things had gotten to the point where they repeated everything she and Joe would say. Joe never had much to say to me. He would tell Nora what he thought or wanted, and she would relay it to me.

Joe always gave them money to go to the movies, but not me. He never gave me a thing. I asked once and he said to me, "Go cut somebody's grass or something," so I did just that, and never asked him again.

When Nora had her telephone installed, she told me, "I don't want you talking on my phone."

The others could use the phone whenever they wanted, and she wouldn't say a word.

One time somebody did call for me, and she started yelling.

"Get off my damned phone! Get off my phone right now! And don't have those kids calling here again. Do you hear me?"

IN THE WOODS

It was cold in the winter of 1961. One day in January or February there was talk of us getting two feet or more of snow. I was just shy of twelve years old. The night before, after Jack, Sean, and I had gone to bed, we could hear Nora and Joe in the living room talking. That's where they slept. Joe was telling her, "If he's not going to school, damn it, get his ass up in the morning and make him go look for a job."

While he was telling her that, Sean and Jack were laughing. They thought it was funny, but I didn't. I stayed awake all night, wondering if she was going to do what he had told her. In fact, I slept in my clothes.

Sure enough, Nora came into the bedroom around 4:30 in the morning.

"Get up, put your clothes on, and go look for a job."

I got up and didn't say a thing. My clothes were already on. When she left the room, Jack and Sean broke into laughter. I put on my shoes and my thin jacket and started walking toward the front door. She started yelling at me as I was going out.

"You don't want to go to school, do you? Just go on out and get a job then, since you want to act like a grownup!"

Again, I said nothing. Joe was there, still in bed, and he remained silent.

I went out the door and started walking down the street in the snow, looking around to see if there was anybody out going to work at that hour of the morning, for I didn't want to be seen.

I was really cold, walking in the snow with shoes that had holes in them. The snow was up to my knees and still falling. I knew I couldn't stay out in the cold too much longer. My hands, ears, and feet were sending painful signals to my brain — signals that I could not ignore. I began to ponder where I could go.

I entered a large apartment building in the neighborhood and went upstairs to the attic to keep warm. I could tell that somebody had been sleeping there. They had spread lots of newspaper all over the cement floor.

I had no desire to go anywhere else, for it was nice and warm in there and I was still shivering. I lay down on the floor in a ball, trying to warm up my body, and dozed off to sleep. I slept until around noon, and then roamed the streets the rest of the day looking for something to eat.

Over the next few days I went into grocery stores and stole various items: lunch meat, ice cream, hot dogs, cookies, cupcakes, anything I could get. I was hungry. I started collecting empty soda bottles and depositing them. I got two cents to a nickel for every small bottle, and as much as a quarter for the large ones. I used the money to buy bologna and bread and whatever else I could afford, and I stole the things I couldn't.

The snow didn't stay around for long. Not far from Nora's place was some woods near a small creek in which I had taken refuge, I dug a hole in the ground, which I used as a place to keep food and the blankets I had picked out of the trash.

I felt that what I was doing was okay as long as nobody knew. At night I went back to that apartment building. I had gotten newspapers, blankets, and rags out of trash cans, which I put down on the cement floor. I would lie down on them roll up in a ball, and go to sleep.

This went on for several weeks, but I eventually got to the point where I didn't think I could go on like this any longer. Things might have been different if it had been during the summer months. I had lost a lot of weight, and I wasn't very big to begin with. My navel protruded by about an inch, giving me one something else to worry about. I didn't know what else to do or where to go, and I didn't care. I just didn't want to go back to Nora's place.

One night while I was roaming the streets, the police stopped me.

"Why are you out here at this time of night?"

"I'm on my way home."

"Where do you live?"

"Two blocks up the street."

"Where up the street?"

At that point I was tempted to run, but the policeman opened his car door.

"Come on, let's go for a ride."

They took me to the police station, where they acknowledged that I was very cold and hungry. They fed me and let me warm up.

"What is your name?"

"Kenzell"

"Kenzell what?"

"Kenzell Evans."

"Kenzell, we can take you to the Receiving Home, or we can take you home. It's up to you."

I didn't want to tell them where home was, for I didn't want to go back there.

"I don't care where you take me."

"Do your parents know you're out here?"

I didn't want to get Nora in trouble.

"No."

"What's your phone number?"

I gave him her number.

He dialed the number.

"Do you have a son named Kenzell Evans?"

"We picked him up off the street tonight. He has no business being out here this time of night, and we're bringing him home. The next time something like this happens it will be reported."

I was happy that they had picked me up, for I was hungry, but I didn't want to go home.

One of the officers said to the other, "Let's take him home." Then he addressed me.

"We're going to give you a break, but don't let us catch you out here again."

I didn't say a thing.

When we got there, the officer knocked and Nora came to the door.

"Where have you been? We've been looking all over for you. What's wrong with you? Are you crazy?"

I just looked at her. I didn't want to embarrass her.

She thanked the officers, and they left.

"Where've you been?"

"What do you mean, where've I been? You told me to get out, to look for a job. Where was I supposed to go?"

"Go in there and wash up. You stink and you're dirty."

Jack and the others were looking at me and laughing. I ignored them. I took a bath and washed out my clothes so I would have something to put on in the morning. I had no other clothes to wear, except an old torn shirt and a pair of pants, and they too were dirty. Nevertheless, I put them on to sleep in.

I went back to school, but before long I stopped attending, for the same reason as before: I had no decent clothes or shoes to wear.

"I'm in junior high school, and I have nothing to wear. I'm tired of wearing the same thing every day. My shoes have no soles, and my clothes are dirty and smelly. Jack and the others don't have to go through any of this. They all have plenty of clothes to wear and a warm coat. Jack has nice shoes and three pairs of pants. He can take gym, but I can't."

Trying to talk to Nora was a waste of time. She didn't care about what I thought or the pressure I was under. She didn't want to hear it.

"You just don't want to go to school. And if you don't go to school, you're not staying here. End of conversation."

She began to sound more and more like Joe. Everything he said she would throw in my face.

On leaving home in the morning, I would roam the streets or go window shopping on Minnesota Avenue. Also, I would collect bottles, and I look for clothes to wear and old blankets to sleep on to keep warm. I found pots and pans to cook in, in case I got put out of Joe and Nora's place again. I knew it was only a matter of time until that happened. I took the blankets, together with everything else I had found, to my little spot in the woods. I found an old wooden box there, put all the things in it, and buried it in the ground next to my food, where nobody would notice or find it.

Every afternoon I made a point of getting home around 3:30, as if I were coming from school. This went on for a while, until one night when Nora came home from work — or from somewhere with Joe — and got me out of bed.

"Get up. Why haven't you been going to school? If you aren't going to go to school, then get yourself a job. You can't stay here. You've got to go."

I don't know how she found out, but that didn't matter. I got up, put my clothes on, and left.

That night it was too cold to sleep in the woods, so I went to my favorite building and up to the attic to keep warm and get some sleep. I got to thinking about my life when all of a sudden I heard someone coming up the steps. It was the maintenance man, and he had a grass sickle in his hands. The sickle swung back, ready to come down on me. I jumped up.

"Damn it! What are you doing up here? Don't you know I could have cut your damned head off? I've been trying to catch those damned winos that have been sleeping up here. I could have killed you! Get out of here, and don't come around here again."

"I won't come back!"

"Go home. Don't you live around here? I've seen you around here before."

I remained silent.

"Get out of here and don't come back."

As I was leaving the building, I saw a boy I knew from school. When he saw me he looked at me as though he knew what was going on. I thought he might have heard the conversation.

"If you say anything about this, I'll whip your ass!"

As it turned out, he apparently didn't know what was going on. Anyhow, I rushed down the street so he wouldn't see how bad I looked. I was dirty. I went to my spot in the woods and went back to sleep.

When I got up later that morning I made a fire and I fixed myself something to eat using the pots I had found. I had eggs, grits, and jelly bread for breakfast, all of which I had bought or stolen from the stores. When I finished I washed out the pots and put them away.

After a few days of roaming the streets looking for bottles, I slowed my pace, hung my head, and started crying, thinking of my mama.

"Mama, help me. Please help me! I don't know what to do."

As soon as I realized I was losing my composure in public, I immediately pulled myself together. I didn't want to be seen that way. I rushed back to my little spot in the woods and cried. After I was all cried out, I just sat there, quietly pondering how to improve my situation. I didn't like living this way.

The following morning the thought of going to the city dump was on my mind instead of roaming the streets. I don't know what had made me think of doing that — perhaps it was Mama's way of answering me — but I was glad I had, for I found lots of shoes. They were everywhere. I was so excited!

There were so many to choose from. Some were too big, and others were too small. It was hard trying to find a matching pair in my size. I didn't have enough time to sort through everything, for I had to get back before school let out and I didn't want anybody to see me. I found a few pair of pants too. I put the pants and the shoes into a large bag, slung it over my shoulder, and left.

When I got back to my spot in the woods I went through the shoes, trying to match them up as best I could. I kept the ones that were too large and stuffed paper into them. They looked funny on me, for I was short. I didn't mind that so much, though I would have preferred smaller shoes, as they would have looked better on my feet.

On the way to the dump, I had noticed a lot of clothes on the clotheslines in one neighborhood. Late that night I went back to that neighborhood, and to my surprise, there was some clothing still hanging out on the lines. I waited to sneak in until I thought everybody was asleep. Then I took my time and got things in my size: four pairs of pants, four shirts, two sweaters, five pairs of socks, some underclothes, and a coat. The coat wasn't all that good, but it was much better than the one I had.

I took only what I needed and left. I started walking faster, knowing I had to stay in the wooded area where I wouldn't be seen. I was so happy that I couldn't wait to get back to my neighborhood and to my spot and get into my new clothes. I started running. I even felt different, imagining how I was going to look wearing the latest styles of pants and shoes. I had a blue pair, a brown pair, and a gray pair of pants, plus a pair of army fatigues, and shirts to go with them.

I couldn't wait to get back in school.

A few days later I was walking down the street and bumped into Nora. She had just gotten off the bus. She looked me up and down.

"Where have you been?"

"Nowhere, you put me out, remember?"

"Why can't you go to school?"

"I want to get back in school."

"Come on, we're going home and I'm going to get you back in school. Where did you get those clothes you have on?"

"One of my friends let me borrow them."

After getting back in school I made stops at my spot in the woods on the way home, where I would get clothes to sneak into the house so I'd have something to wear the next day.

"Where did you get those clothes?"

"I told you, I borrowed them from a friend."

The gym instructor was impressed with my athletic ability, especially in track and field. He tried to encourage me to run track.

"You're a natural runner, and you're real fast. With your speed, we want you on our track team."

I loved to run, but I didn't know how to tell him I didn't have decent shoes to run in. I was a proud kid but by now I was quiet, for I was ashamed of the way I was living and didn't want anyone to know.

"I'll think about it."

I couldn't run or jump in the shoes I was wearing. I wanted to and tried many times, but I would end up stopping for the pain was too severe. The large shoes caused blisters to form, and my skin would rub off when I tried to run or play ball. The small shoes were so tight that I had to fold my toes down at times. That caused corns to develop on my toes, eight on each foot, my toenails started growing crooked and sideways. Sometimes I could barely walk, but I did it when I was around other people. I tried to act normal. As time went on I got used to wearing the shoes, but my feet continued to hurt.

HARD CRIME

Just when I thought things were getting better, they took a turn for the worse.

Sean had been taking coins from Joe's dresser drawer — coins Joe had been saving since he was in the army — to use in the candy and gum machines. Everybody in the family except Nora and Joe had seen Sean with Joe's coins. Indeed, Sean had told us what he was doing with them. He had taken Joe's watch too. He was good at taking things apart and trying to put them back together.

One day in July of 1962, Joe came home and noticed that his watch was missing. He came straight toward me and hit me hard on the side of my head with his fist.

"Where is my damn watch? I told you to keep your hands off my shit. Don't be touching my things."

"I didn't touch your watch. I don't know what you're talking about. I haven't touched anything of yours."

"You're a liar! Nobody but you got into my things!"

He hit me again, and I instinctively hit him back, in the face, twice as hard as I thought I was capable of. The fight was on!

We started indoors and ended up in the backyard, where the neighbors could see. The fight went on for a good while. I was taking all of my anger and frustration out on him.

Patrice jumped on my back, yelling "Leave my daddy alone! Leave my daddy alone!" She was pulling me and hitting me as we fought.

Nora came outside, shouting "Break it up! Break it up!" She got in between us.

"You should be ashamed of yourself! You had no business messing with his things. Go on. Leave. Just leave!"

"I know nothing about his things. I didn't touch his stuff."

The others were right there, but nobody said a word in my defense. And neither Joe nor Nora questioned them as to who had taken the watch.

I went back inside to get my things.

"Where are you going? I said leave."

"I'm going to get my clothes."

"You get them and leave."

I got my clothes, and as I was leaving, Nora spoke again.

"You're the one who did it. Why are you always messing with Joe's stuff anyway?"

"If he ever puts his hands on me again, I'll kill him. I mean it."

At that point I left. The next time they saw me was months later.

I stayed in school as long as I could, eventually I drop out again, and I started hanging out on street corners with my new friends, drinking wine and partying. I eventually became a member of a gang. It was there that I learned how to play cards and shoot dice, how to boost and shoot pool. My life was changing fast.

One night a few of us went to a party in the neighborhood. We couldn't get in, so we started throwing bricks through the windows. Afterwards we split up I headed for my spot in the woods. As I was walking down the street, four guys ran up to me.

"Who threw those bricks through the windows?"

"What windows?"

As we were talking, I could see the pearl handle of a gun coming out of his pocket. I hit him as hard as I could, and he fell to the ground. Then I took off running. As I was running, I could hear gunshots.

Bang! Bang! Bang!

"I'm going to kill that MF! I'm going to kill him!"

I thought I had been hit, for my back was burning. I ran through somebody's yard and dived into some tall hedges. The guys who were pursuing me ran right past me. I lay there until I thought they were gone. Then I got up and went to Joe's sister's house. She had moved from North Carolina long before I did. She was nice and lived in the area too, but she didn't know what was going on at home and I didn't tell her.

I knocked on her door.

"Who is it?"

"Barney."

I could see that she was looking through the peephole. Then she opened the door.

"Barney, what are you doing out here at this time of night? Does your mama know you're out here?"

"Yeah, I was leaving a friend's house and walking down the street when some guys started shooting at me. I think I've been shot."

"Come on in and take off your jacket and your shirt."

I stepped inside and took off my jacket. I saw that there were holes in it across the back. Then I took off my shirt, and it was bloody in the back.

"You haven't been shot. You were creased across the back. What are you doing out here at this time of night?"

"As I told you, I was leaving a friend's house and heading for home."

"Let me bandage you up, and then you can go home."

The next day I found out where the guy lived and hung out. I got a gun from one of my friends and went into his neighborhood looking for him. After several trips, I left word with his friends that I was looking for him, but I never caught up with him.

I made a lot of new friends, including a guy by the name of Willie Gray. We became close friends.

Willie was big boned and fat. He had a dark brown complexion and big eyes. His black hair was cut short, and tapered in the front and on the sides. He was about 5'8" in height and weighed about 195 pounds.

He lived in Northwest Washington[1] with his mother. I spent the night at their house many times. It was a godsend to finally have a place to stay where my presence was not likely to arouse suspicion.

One Friday evening Willie and I had been drinking with some friends on the corner. One of them said, "I heard there's supposed to be a party tonight at the church."

Willie and I decided to walk over to the church. When we got there, some guys from another gang were trying to get in too. All of us had been drinking. Somehow we got into a fight. It didn't last very long, as the other guys immediately started running toward the church. Some of their

---

1 Washington, D.C. is divided into four quadrants: Northwest, Northeast, Southwest, and Southeast. In street addresses their names are abbreviated as N.W., N.E., S.W., and S.E., respectively.

friends were in there, opening the door and sneaking them in. I picked up a brick.

"The next one to open that door is going to get it."

When the door opened, I threw the brick. After the air had cleared, I saw that I had hit the priest in the head. Everybody scattered. There were several people there who knew Willie and me and had seen me throw the brick.

I spent three months in the Receiving Home.

When they released me I went right back to the streets and joined my friends. By this time they had outgrown me. That didn't bother me, but there were a few times when I wondered what they were eating. I was only 5'5" and weighed about 120 pounds, and they all beat me on both counts.

I saw Willie later that day.

"I lost my mother while you were gone."

"I'm sorry to hear that. Are you okay?"

"Yeah, man, I'm okay."

Now it seemed as though everywhere I went, people were talking about drugs or taking it or at least talking about doing so. It was as if a strong wind had come along and brought the drug culture with it. It was in all the neighborhoods. My friends were users. And if you weren't a user, you weren't hip.

Some of my friends had a drug habit and were willing to shoot just about anything into their bodies as long as they could feel something. I started smoking weed and snorting right along with them. I wanted to see what they were feeling and what they were getting out of it. I didn't find it all that exciting. It didn't make me feel particularly good. I thought that perhaps I was missing something, so I asked a friend who lived around the corner from me about it. His name was Butch. We had gone to school together a couple years ago.

"What am I supposed to feel? The weed makes me laugh, act silly, and feel paranoid, and it gives me the munchies."

"Man, that's an upper. You don't need that. You're already hyper. You need some drop, something to slow you down. That'll make you nod and put you in the groove."

"What groove?"

"I can't explain it to you, try shooting it."

One evening I was walking down the street and saw Butch coming in my direction.

"Hey man, I just copped. You wanta get high?"

"If it's free, cause I ain't got no money."

"Yeah, come on."

We started walking to his house. His parents hadn't gotten home yet.

"You hit me first, because I don't know how to do it."

"Come on."

He stuck the needle in my arm. After a few seconds I said, "Okay, take it out. Take it out!" He didn't take it out right then. I fell to my knees.

"I'm getting dizzy. Take it out. I feel as if I'm going to pass out. I can hardly breathe. Take it out."

I was gasping.

"Is it good? Is it good?"

"Take it out!"

Butch finally took out the needle and helped me up.

"I need to walk."

We started walking around in his yard. I could barely breathe, and I felt as if I was going to pass out. I felt helpless, losing control over myself.

"Come on, let's walk around the block."

We walked around the block several times, with him holding me up. I was dragging along, and he was trying to keep me awake. I kept putting my finger in my mouth in an effort to throw up. After I succeeded in doing that, we started walking faster in the hope that it would help clear my head. When it did start to clear I said, "Shit. I thought I was a goner."

From that day on I never shot drugs again. That was my first and last time. I did snort on one or two occasions, but I never shot anything into my arms.

One day I was out with some friends and they were snorting dope.

"Do you want a hit, man?"

"No. Y'all can have that shit. That's not for me."

"Come on, man. Stop acting like that."

"Nope, you can have it. I don't get anything out of it."

Most of the guys were older than I. They hung out around the liquor store, the carryout, or the barber shop, begging for money to get something to eat or drink, or to get a haircut that they could brag about. It wasn't that big a deal to me. Everybody wore their hair short to hide the naps, myself included.

I thought I could learn something from being around them, but they didn't know as much as I did. They were weak minded. I also realized they were followers, just like nearly everyone who had gotten caught up in the drug culture.

I moved on. I never stayed around anybody for long. Being on the move was my way of keeping people out of my business. The only thing anyone ever really found out about me was that I lived in Northeast. I never talked about my personal life, and people very seldom asked. When they did, I just said I didn't want to talk about it. And that would be the end of it. I was ashamed of the direction my life was taking.

I made two new friends, John and Smelly. John was a tall, skinny guy, with a peanut head and big lips. Smelly was tall too and had a medium build, a big head, and protruding ears. His face was flat, like a pie. He was always smiling.

Actually, they weren't new. I had met them when I was in the Receiving Home. They were members of a gang from upper Northwest.

We started sticking up drug dealers, taking their money and drugs. We wore ski masks and dark shades whenever we did this, so we wouldn't be recognized, and we never called one another by name. John would get a rental car for us to do our dirty work in, and we would put out-of-town tags on them — tags that we had stolen.

We divided up everything among the three of us. John and Smelly would take the drugs to somebody they knew in either Southeast or Northeast who didn't use the stuff and would in turn sell it. We would get half the money. Their names were never mentioned. I stayed out of the picture for that part of the operation. I didn't know the guys and didn't want to know them. I let John and Smelly handle that.

One night we came close to killing a big-time drug dealer during a robbery that almost went bad. We had heard that he was into bragging, and we plotted how to rob him. Once we found out where he lived, we got a small gas can and filled it with gasoline and some duct tape. We went to his house and waited for him to come home.

When he did, we rushed in on him. He had no idea what was happening. We had taken him totally by surprise. When he realized what was happening he tried to buck.

"You don't know who you're fucking with. Do you know who I am?"

"We know who you are. We came for the money and drugs."

"I'm not giving you shit. You young niggers had better get the fuck out of here."

He started getting loud and tried to reach for his gun, which was under a sofa pillow. John had a gun in his hand, and Smelly had a pike. John started beating him with his pistol, and Smelly hit him in the head with the pike. He fell to the floor.

I got a washcloth, soaked it in gasoline, stuffed it into his mouth, and covered it with duct tape to keep him quiet, and I taped his arms to his sides. Then I poured gasoline all over him and lit a match, fully intending to throw it on him, but at that point he started moaning. I removed part of the tape from his mouth.

"Are you trying to say something?"

"Please! Please! Don't kill me. You can have it. You can have everything. I won't squeal on you. Just don't set me on fire. Please don't set me on fire!"

"Where's the money and dope?"

"It's in the closet, in a safe under those clothes. The combination is 39-00-34. Please don't set me on fire! I promise I won't tell anyone."

We took what we had come for and left him on the floor crying, soaked in gasoline, as we went out the door.

Once we got into the car, nobody said a word until we were a good distance from the guy's house.

"Were you really going to set him on fire?"

"Wasn't that the plan if he bucked? If he had gotten to that gun, he would have shot one or more of us, and perhaps even killed us."

It got silent.

"Hey man, I saw some black and white FootJoy shoes. I'm going to get me a pair tomorrow."

"Where did you see them?"

"Warner's Shoe Store."

"I'm going to get me a brown pair."

"Well, I guess I'll get the brown and white ones."

All three of us dressed nicely, and every time we were seen we had on a different outfit. Smelly and John spent a lot of their money at nightclubs, where they had a good time splurging on girls. They also hung out in the pool halls uptown.

I couldn't hang out in those places with them. I was too young. I wasn't interested anyway. I wasn't into all of that, nor did I care for that kind of attention. I saved most of my money and always went back to my spot in the woods and buried it. While I was there I thought about school and what I was doing with my life. I wasn't happy with the direction my life was taking. It wasn't what I really wanted. I felt I had to make a change for the better.

One day I met a man who owned a pool hall, and he let me in even though I wasn't old enough. Everybody called him J. D. He was a tall guy, well built, and weighed about 220 pounds. And he had had his hair straightened.

One day he needed to change a hundred-dollar bill, but nobody had change for it. I walked over to him.

"You need change for a hundred?"

He looked at me with curiosity in his eyes.

"Yeah, do you have change?"

I reached into my pocket and pulled out a roll of money.

"Yeah, here you are."

I handed him five twenty-dollar bills and walked away. At first he was speechless. Then he walked over to me.

"You forgot your hundred-dollar bill."

"I didn't forget. It's just my way of thanking you."

"Thanking me for what?"

"For letting me come in here."

"Where did you get all that money?"

"I'm a hustler."

"What do you do?"

"Nothing, I just talk to people."

"That's fine with me."

A week or so later, J. D. started giving me lessons in how to shoot pool. We would do this after he closed up for the night.

"What's your name?"

"My name is Kenzell."

"I've always wanted a son like you, cool and calm."

"I can change, you know."

"I know. I've been watching you. Are you okay?"

"I'm okay."

"Why aren't you in school?"

"I plan to go back."

"That's good. Don't throw your life away."

"I'm not going to."

"I notice you don't come around much anymore. What are you doing with your time these days?"

"I don't like people asking me questions about being here, for I'm too young. I appreciate your letting me in, but I'm about to give this up and try to get back in school."

"That's good. If you're ever here and someone questions you about your age, just say that I'm your father. Is that okay with you?"

"Sure. Thanks."

About a week later, John, Smelly, and I were talking.

"I'm not going to be doing this anymore."

"What's wrong, man?"

"This isn't the kind of thing I want to be doing for the rest of my life. Besides, I'm going back to school."

"We have a good thing going on."

"I've already made up my mind."

"Well, I guess we'll have to find another guy."

"I know who we can get: Robert. He's cool, and he isn't into the drug scene. All he does is hustle. He'll be glad to work with us."

"What do you think?"

"I have nothing to do with it, nor do I want to know what you guys decide. Just be careful."

They knew nothing about me, other than that I lived in Northeast and was a member of another gang. I knew things about them besides their gang involvement. I was on their turf, and had been there most of the time.

As time went on I started drifting away from them. Eventually I quit hanging out with them altogether.

NORA AND STEREO

I went back to living with Nora and Joe, and I got back in school — a vocational school, which I attended in the evenings. This time I had clothes to wear. I still had my spot in the woods, where I kept my clothes and money and other belongings in case they put me out again.

I was fourteen, but I lied about my age and got a day job working at a little grocery store that I had formerly stolen food from — and still was stealing from, every chance I got. I made about $22 a week and had to give Nora $15 of that for rent. She constantly reminded me, "You can't stay here for nothing. You'll have to pay rent."

At the age of fifteen I again lied about my age, claiming that I was sixteen, and took the Civil Service exam, which I passed. Shortly thereafter I received a letter from Goddard Space Flight Center, saying that I was to report for work on such and such a day. I didn't know where that was, so I asked Nora.

"I got a job offer. Do you know where Goddard Space Flight Center is?"

"No. Get out of my face."

She didn't offer to help me find out where it was, so I asked someone at work one day.

"Do you know where Goddard Space Flight Center is?"

"Yeah, it's in Greenbelt, Maryland. It's a long way from here, and no buses go out there."

I decided not to pursue that opportunity, but I didn't give up looking for a job, a real job. I looked everywhere. I needed to make more money to get the things I wanted. I was sick of hearing Nora's complaints about

37

my not giving her enough money. I told no one about the money I was saving, and I wasn't about to spend it.

About two weeks later I got a job as a dishwasher at a George Washington University cafeteria, at Nineteenth and F streets, N.W. It was my first real job, and I again lied about my age to get it. I quit the job at the grocery store.

The job paid about $1.15 an hour. My take-home pay was about $40 to $45 a week, including some overtime. I was so relieved that I could finally buy my own clothes and get the things I wanted, without having to hide them, and that I would no longer have to deal with the pressure I had felt before.

When I brought home my first paycheck I was so excited that I could hardly wait to tell Nora. I was expecting her to be happy for me, but as it turned out I was in for a big shock.

"How much money did you make?"

"I made $42."

"You'll have to give me $30 a week. I need more money to pay bills. Joe isn't working right now."

I was speechless. I didn't expect Nora to demand that much of my pay. Now I wouldn't be able to buy the clothes I had counted on getting.

I was able to put a few things on lay-a-way, but before long Nora made me give her $35 a week. Essentially the amount left over I got to keep, about $7, I needed for bus fare to get to and from work. I was always willing to work over time.

Jack was working too, at Miss Ray's Diner, where Nora worked. She had gotten him a job there long before I got a job, and he didn't have to give her a red cent. She never asked him for money, and he was allowed to do anything he wanted with his pay.

After being back in school for a few months I decided to drop out. Nora was getting most of my money, and I needed to work more overtime hours to get the things I wanted.

My focus on school wasn't with me anymore. I felt I wasn't getting anything out of it. I was there just in body, not in mind. I had lost all interest in school. It was about survival for me now. I felt I was wasting not only my own time but everybody else's as well.

I announced my decision to Nora.

"I'm dropping out of school. I'm no longer getting anything out of it. There's too much pressure on me, and I can't concentrate on my schoolwork. The harder I try, the harder it gets. I just can't take it anymore."

"Oh, you just don't *want* to go. That's your problem. You just don't want to do *anything*. If you do drop out of school, don't think you're going to live here for nothing."

"I put clothes on lay-a-way that I can't pay for, because you're taking all my money. And now I've lost the chance to buy them."

"Boy, go somewhere and get out of my face."

Shortly thereafter I got a job at a warehouse that distributed toys to various stores in the D.C. metropolitan area. I quit the job at George Washington, for this job paid more money. I didn't tell Nora, however, as she would have taken more of my pay.

During the Christmas season — actually, all during the months of October, November and December — everybody at the warehouse was busy filling orders placed by the stores. That's what I did.

I got to know a guy who lived in my neighborhood and worked there. He drove one of the delivery trucks. His name was Bill. We became good friends. Bill was a tall, slim, light-skinned man. He was in his 30s, married, with five kids. He also had a car. Together, we came up with a scheme to steal some of the toys.

He gave me a list of all the toys he wanted for his kids. I didn't have a list for myself. I just wanted as many talking dolls, lionel train sets, and battery-powered cars as I could get. They were the newest toys, the ones that everybody was talking about. I knew I could make them more affordable to parents.

I would load our stuff on the truck first and then pack it with the merchandise for the store orders. At the end of the day, Bill would drop our stuff off at his house. Besides that, he would leave his car keys with me. Every chance I got, I stole additional toys from the warehouse and loaded them into the trunk of his car, until it was filled up. After work I would ride home with him and pick up the toys I intended to sell.

People were buying toys from me as fast as I could get them. I always had about $600 to $700 in my pocket. In fact, I was so busy that I often didn't get around to cashing my checks right away. When I did cash them, I bought clothes and started putting furniture on lay-a-way at the Hub Furniture Store, one of the largest furniture stores in the city I thought.

I didn't even have anywhere to put furniture. I bought it only because I remembered roaming the streets and going window shopping when I was younger, and I recalled the images that had formed in my mind back then—images of the kind of house I wanted and of how I would furnish it.

Sometimes I took all the money I had left over after giving Nora her $35, and I put it toward paying for the furniture I had on lay-a-way. I had also taken all the money from my place in the woods and used it to pay for furniture. I kept only about $10 on hand for other things. I always knew I would have more in a few days, for I had a long list of names of people who I was seeing on their payday.

I couldn't tell Nora what I was doing, for if she knew she would demand that I give her even more of my pay each week. All she wanted was money. She hadn't shown me any affection since the day she brought me to D.C. to live with her.

Quite often I didn't go straight home, since there was almost never anything for me to eat at Nora's place. She and Joe and their kids usually ate up all the food before I got there. Most times I stopped at a carryout and got myself something to eat. At other times I just roamed the streets or went to my spot in the woods. One night Nora questioned me about this.

"Why didn't you eat anything?"

"What would I have eaten? You know you don't save anything for me."

"Why do you get home so late? You should come home right after work and have dinner with us. You pretend to be a grownup, but you aren't."

"I feel as if I am a grownup, because I'm paying my own way."

"Why don't you call me Mama, like all the others?"

"You don't treat me the same way you treat them. I've felt unwanted ever since I got here. If people were to see us in the street, they wouldn't know we were kin, because we don't associate with each other.

"You and Joe make me feel as if I'm not good enough for y'all, as if there's something wrong with me. And that has sent your other kids a message that it's okay for them to treat me the same way that y'all do. You and Joe act as if you're living in a fantasy world with your four golden kids. I say four, not five, because y'all mistreat Kim as well, and calling her Buckwheat. It's hard for me to live under the same roof with y'all and try to feel accepted."

"I treat all of y'all the same. You can ask them. They'll tell you."

"I'm sure they will," I replied sarcastically. Then I just stood there and looked at her, without uttering another word.

Two weeks later I was walking through the furniture store when it occurred to me that I could be of help to Nora by buying something nice for her.

I decided to get her a stereo system. The one I picked out cost over $500. I was so excited that I could hardly wait to see her reaction.

When I got home the next day, I saw that it had already been delivered.

"How did you get this?"

"I bought it for you. Do you like it?"

She didn't say a word. She just looked at it and never even thanked me. At that moment I realized that all she wanted was money. And I could see that she was incapable of expressing gratitude to anyone, not just me.

After the newness of the stereo system had worn off, I wasn't allowed to touch it, but it was okay for the others to do so.

Nora had never had any new furniture. That was the only decent piece of furniture she had.

Joe had never tried to do anything to better himself. It appeared that there was nothing he really wanted, because he showed no ambition. His entire world consisted of drinking liquor and hanging out with his friends. Nora didn't drink, but, always playing cards and numbers games.

Shortly thereafter Jack got locked up, but I never knew what for. They never spoke of it in my presence, and I neither asked nor cared.

MEETING MARGIE

In the summer of 1965 I met a girl by the name of Margie Ward. She was fifteen years old, a year younger than I. She was in high school and would be entering tenth grade in the fall.

Margie was working a summer job with the D.C. Recreation Board. She worked with kids at a church. When I first laid eyes on her I thought she was very attractive. She had a stylish hair cut — and tapered at the back of her neck. She was short, about 5'5", and weighed about 104 pounds. She had smooth brown skin and a nice shape, with pretty white teeth and a beautiful smile to go with them.

We started seeing each other as often as possible. I fell in love with her. One day as I was coming down the street toward her house, she saw me and started running toward me, with her arms outstretched and a big smile on her face, anticipating a big hug and a kiss from me. I was trying to be cool as I walked toward her, looking around and feeling embarrassed.

"What's wrong with you? Put your arms down."

"I'm happy to see you! Give me a hug and a kiss!"

"Stop playing girl, stop playing. We're out in public."

She wouldn't stop. She was all over me.

"So what if we're out in public? You're my baby! Now give me a big hug and a big kiss, and I'll leave you alone!"

I didn't know what to say. I gave her a hug and a kiss, and as we walked back to her house I said,

"I'm not used to getting this kind of affection."

In my heart that's what I wanted, but I hadn't had it in years. It made me think of my Mama, who had truly cared for me.

I thought about Nora and Joe and their kids, they never showed any affection, and now for the first time I realized that their lack of affection was rubbing off on me.

Meeting Margie had made me feel as though somebody cared about me and wanted me. I felt better when I was around her, though I didn't know how to accept the affection she was showing me. In fact, I felt that I had robbed her of her natural tendency to express her affection for me in public, for she never again did that with me.

Her parents were separated. She lived with her father. She had a sister and two younger brothers. Her father's name was Spencer Ward. He was dark skinned and had a muscular build. Looking as if he had been a ball player, he was about 5'9" and weighed about 200 pounds, and had had his hair straightened. He carried himself like a playboy, and drove a little sports car.

Margie's sister's name was Barbara. She was a nice-looking girl, light skinned, about 5'6" in height, and she weighed about 110 pounds. She was in her last year of junior high school. Everything struck her as funny. I thought she was a little off.

The older of Margie's two brothers was named Jasper. He was tall, but not as tall as his father. He had a small frame and looked as if he wasn't getting enough to eat.

The other brother was named Lewis, a little fat boy. He lived with their grandmother, Theresa Ward. She was a short, dark-skinned lady, about 5'5" and on the heavy side, weighing about 165 pounds. She lived in Maryland and worked in D.C.

I didn't know much about Margie's mother, other than that she lived in D.C. with her boyfriend.

Her father and I got along pretty well. He would invite me over for dinner and often told me about the social club to which he belonged, which didn't interest me in the least. We never really talked about anything important. I knew he was checking me out, so I didn't say anything.

Being that I was the quiet type and had always kept my business to myself, one day he broached a subject that I had been dreading.

"What do you do?"

"I work during the day and go to school in the evening."

I lied. I didn't want Margie's father to think ill of me for being a dropout, and I didn't want to take the chance of losing her. He didn't know much about me, other than that I was seeing his daughter, and that I was young and dressed nicely and kept money in my pocket.

He then found out that I had been buying his daughter nice clothes and expensive shoes. That was okay with him, because he couldn't afford clothes like that and with his lifestyle.

He drove through the neighborhood asking questions about me.

He knew that his daughter and I were spending a lot of time together, and he never disapproved. In fact, he welcomed me. Everybody in Margie's family took to me.

That allowed me to feel accepted, something I had been deprived of for some time. It made me feel wanted and gave me a sense of being a part of something. Nevertheless, I kept these feelings to myself.

I went over one evening after work, and Margie was outside sitting on the steps with her head down. I walked up to her.

"Hey, what's up?"

She looked up at me.

"Hi."

She looked glum.

"What's wrong?"

"Nothing, I'm okay."

"Baby, you can't fool me. I can tell something's wrong. What is it?"

"My girlfriend came to visit me and Daddy sent me to the store, claiming that he wanted to talk to her alone. By the time I got back, he had raped her."

"How do you know?"

"I walked in on them."

"Where were Barbara and Jasper while this was going on?"

"They were with my grandmother."

"What did your girlfriend say?"

"She didn't say anything. He's dating her mother too. She comes around here from time to time. You've never seen her."

"No, I haven't. Do she live around here?"

"Not too far from here."

"Are you okay?"

"I guess so. I'm upset that he did that to my friend."

"Maybe she wanted it, since she didn't say anything."

"He has a lot of girlfriends that he brings to the house."

"This is his house, isn't it?"

"He didn't have to do that to my friend."

"I agree with on that, she's under age. You said she didn't say anything, so she must have wanted it too."

44

Margie didn't respond, so I changed the subject.

"Let's go to the movies."

"What are we going to see?"

"I don't care. Anything would be fine with me."

We never talked about that again.

About a month later, Willie and I were together one day and I introduced him to Barbara, and they started seeing each other.

Margie and I had been together for over two years, and things were going pretty well. Then on a warm July day in 1967 she informed me of something that was bothering her.

"I'm scared. I didn't have a period this month. I might be pregnant. I don't know what to do."

"You don't have to be scared. I'm not scared. I'm happy, and I'm happy for you. Everything will be fine."

I was actually excited! I had never told Margie how I was treated at home, and she had never asked. She just assumed everything was normal. I felt that this was my opportunity to finally get away from Nora and Joe and have a family of my own.

I knew it was going to be a boy. I just knew it. When I was alone I often thought of how my life was changing. I made a vow to myself that my son wouldn't go through what I had been through, and that I would set him on the right path.

That was the most important thing on my mind: getting myself together and becoming a good father to my as-yet-unborn son.

I was elated when I found out that Margie was pregnant, she didn't share that feeling. She was worried about her father's reaction and afraid she'd have to drop out of school, and she was trying to figure out how she was going to tell him. I said to her, "Don't worry about a thing. Everything will be all right. We'll break the news to your father when he gets home from work this evening."

Seconds later the door opened, and he came in.

"Hi baby. Hey Kenzell!"

"Hi Daddy."

"Mr. Ward, we need to talk to you."

"Okay, give me a minute."

He walked into the back room, put his things down, and then came into the living room and sat down.

"Margie is pregnant."

"I had a feeling."

I was relieved to know that, but I had no idea what he thought about his daughter's becoming pregnant while she was still in high school.

"I'll take care of her and the baby."

"I believe you will. Baby, you can still finish school. Don't worry about a thing. You're going to be okay."

"Thank you, Daddy."

I felt better, knowing she felt relieved.

"Thanks."

"You're going to be all right, man."

I later got a job with the D.C. school system, working the night shift. I was still working at the warehouse too, but business there had slowed down. I worked both jobs and saved my money.

The furniture I had originally picked out was paid for, but I decided to get something better instead.

Mr. Wilson worked at the furniture store. An older man, in his fifties, he was the sales manager and the person I always talked to when I went there.

He said, "Hello, Mr. Evans. When and where would you like to have your furniture delivered?"

I didn't have a place to put it.

"I've decided that I want to get something different. I don't want that furniture anymore. I let it stay on lay-a-way too long. Besides, I want something better."

"Mr. Evans, you have done this sort of thing twice before. Don't you have a good idea of the kind of furniture you're looking for?"

"I like contemporary furniture, brand-name merchandise, and I want something new, not something that's already been out on the showroom floor. I want some furniture of higher quality."

"Let me get some catalogs for you to look through."

He came back with a stack of catalogs.

"Perhaps you can find what you want in one of these. They're all from brand-name manufacturers. Their merchandise is of high quality, but it isn't cheap. And by the way, stereo systems are now making way for new systems called component sets. We have two of them on the floor, over there. If you'd like, we can take a look at them. I also have a catalog with additional component sets."

I briefly looked through one of the catalogs.

"Mr. Evans, we can get you anything you want. We can't stock it, because most people can't afford it. I'm a lot older than you, and I can't afford it myself."

"This is exactly the kind of thing I'm interested in."

"All right, I'm going to leave you alone. Take your time picking out what you want, and let me know when you're ready."

When I finished I got Mr. Wilson's attention, and he came over.

"I think I've hit on the right merchandise this time. I marked everything I want."

"Let's see what you marked. Oh, this is really nice! You have good taste."

"Did I forget something?"

"I don't think so."

Nobody knew about the furniture, not even Margie. And I wouldn't dare tell Nora, because I wouldn't have anything left by the time she got finished with it. I kept my plans to myself.

I bought Margie maternity clothes, and was always there for her in case she needed anything. Nobody had to buy anything, and I didn't expect them to. I made sure she had everything she needed before the baby was born.

I bought a crib, a high chair, a stroller, and a bassinet, as well as plenty of baby bottles and formula, baby clothes, and diapers. Margie's bedroom and living room were nearly stacked to the ceiling.

Her family, especially her grandmother and her father, couldn't believe all the things I had bought. They were busy trying to figure out where I had gotten the money to buy them.

I walked in the door one day and her father was saying to her, "I'm very happy for you. You should be thankful for having somebody to care for you the way he does. He's a good guy. That's a man for you! A lot of guys wouldn't have done this."

About a month later Margie brought up the subject of marriage.

"My father and my grandmother keep telling me we should get married before the baby is born, so the baby won't be called a bastard."

"They're pressuring you, and I suppose they expect you to put pressure on me. I don't particularly like that."

"Can we get married?"

"I've never thought about getting married. That's never been an issue with me. I don't want to make a hasty decision about it, one way or the other, but I promise you I'll think about it."

During the following week or so I thought about it a lot. I knew it was bothering Margie, Things had been better than what I've had in the past. Besides, being married might make me feel I'm a part of something, that I'm doing something with my life.

I was at her house one evening and we decided to go for a walk.

"Okay, we'll get married."

"I'm so happy. I love you so much, Kenzell. I'm going to be a good wife to you and a good mother to our baby. I promise."

"Now you can tell your father and your grandmother so they can stop pressuring you."

"I will!"

Neither Margie nor anyone in her family knew my family, and they didn't ask about them. That was fine with me, because I didn't want them to know what kind of people they were or how I had lived.

I did tell Nora that I was getting married.

"Boy, you get out of my face. Any girl who would want you has got to be crazy."

It was on the fourth of April of that year, 1968 that the news flash appeared on TV.

"Martin Luther King Jr. has been assassinated."

The city of Washington was in an uproar. Rioting was going on everywhere. The looting went on for two or three days. Willie and I were right in the center of it, taking anything and everything that we could use. A curfew had gone into effect around 6 p.m., but a lot of people were still out on the streets. The National Guard was called in to protect businesses.

The last store we went into was a liquor store in our neighborhood. We met another man while we were in there. He was getting liquor and beer for himself.

"If you guys help me carry my cases home, I'll let y'all stash yours at my house until things cool down."

"Where do you live, and how many cases do you have?"

"I live right around the corner, less than 80 yards from here. We can go through the alley. That's shorter. I have twenty cases left."

"It's a deal."

"How much are y'all taking?"

"All we can, but only the liquor in the cases."

"Okay, I'm ready when y'all are."

"We're ready. We can take two to three cases at a time. We'll follow you.

When we got to his house I said, "You can just stay here and make some room for our stuff."

"Are you sure? I can help."

"There's no need for you to go along with us, we got it."

When we started walking back to the store, Willie said, "Why did you tell him to stay home? He could have helped us."

"He *is* helping. He's making room for us to store our stuff at his place. Let's concentrate on getting the rest of the stuff out of the store as fast as we can, before somebody sees us and cut us short."

We went back into the store, and Willie saw a tall hand truck.

"This is just what we need. I can carry seven cases at a time with it. Yeah, we'll have this over with in no time."

"That's what I'm talking about. I can take at lease three cases. After another trip we'll be done with his, and we can start working on ours."

After about five more trips we were leaving with our last load, when four guys ran into the store. We came out with forty to fifty cases of liquor. We stacked ours against the basement wall in the man's house and gave him the hand truck.

When we went back later on to get our liquor, we gave the man another six cases, and Willie said, "That was an easy hustle."

"We have to get rid of it. We can't drink all of it ourselves. We have to figure out who we're going to sell it to."

We later sold some to a few bootleggers and the rest to owners of other liquor stores.

MY SON

$\mathcal{O}n$ the $evening$ of April 9, 1968 I decided to call Margie's house to check on her and see if she was okay, for I knew it would soon be time for her to give birth.

Barbara said, "I have been trying to get in touch with you all morning. Margie had the baby. It's a boy! Grandma is over there with her now."

"Damn! Okay, I'll talk with you later. I'm on my way to the hospital."

I rushed over to D.C. General Hospital to see her and the baby.

When I got there, Mrs. Ward was still there, holding the baby. Margie and the baby were both fine.

"Isn't he a cute little baby?"

I didn't say a word. I just looked at him.

Then Mrs. Ward handed Margie the baby.

"I think he's hungry."

Margie proceed to breastfeed him, and was happy to see me.

"Look at him. Isn't he cute? Isn't he handsome? I named him Kenzell, after you. I don't know how you feel about that, since we've never talked about a name. We can change it if there's another name you would prefer."

I stood up and took a close look at the baby.

"Well, I can live with the name Kenzell, I'll call him Junior, but he doesn't look handsome to me."

Margie's face dropped.

"Don't say that."

"Well, you asked me, and I'm telling you."

50

I was actually as happy as could be, and unable to hold back a smile any longer.

About ten minutes later her father and Barbara came into the room.

"Congratulations," said her father as he smiled at me.

"Thanks."

"Congratulations, Dad."

I just smiled.

They were trying to decide who he resembled most. "He's cute. He looks like you."

"He doesn't look like anyone but himself. I don't think he's so cute and handsome. He looks ugly to me. As far as I know, they could have switched babies."

"Oh no, he's yours! He looks like you."

"No way, I'm handsome, and he's ugly. He doesn't look like me. I don't know who he looks like."

I was actually very happy, but I didn't want to show it.

A few days later, Margie and the baby came home. Her girlfriends had given her a surprise welcome home party. I bought cigars and passed them out to everybody.

Soon thereafter I started looking for an apartment. I wanted to have a place of my own. The money I was giving Nora for rent could go toward my own rent if I had an apartment. I was making enough money now. Besides, I'd never been happy living with them.

While looking for an apartment, I ran into an old friend of mine by the name of Ron. We had met while hanging out in the pool hall and had become good friends. He was a decent kind of guy.

"How you doing, man?"

"I'm okay, man. How you been?"

"I'm okay, trying to get myself together. I got me a place in Maryland. You got to come visit me and check it out."

"I will. I'm looking for a place now too. Give me your address. Oh, I forgot to mention that I just became the father of a little boy!"

"Congratulations! Where's my cigar?"

"You're too late for that."

He handed me a piece of paper with his address and phone number on it.

"I'm just kidding. I wish you luck in finding a place. And sorry for rushing, man, but I have to get to work and I have a stop to make first. By the way, where are you working?"

"I work with the D.C. school system."

"I'm working for the school system in Prince George's County. They're hiring now, and they pay more than D.C. You should check them out."

Prince George's County is in Maryland and borders on D.C.

"I will. Thanks, man. I'll check them out."

"You do that, man. I'll talk with you later."

I went there the same day and filled out an application. I had quit the job at the warehouse a few months earlier, for the work had slowed down so much.

Within a few days I found an apartment, a one-bedroom place, not too far from where Margie lived. The building was under management of a firm by the name of William A. Smith, so I went to their rental office downtown and applied. They were located at Seventh Street and Massachusetts Avenue, N.W.

"You're too young. You need a co-signer, or at least good credit."

I wanted this apartment so badly. It rented for only $70 a month. I was giving Nora $35 a week for rent and getting essentially nothing for it. I had to get this apartment. I didn't want to ask Nora to co-sign for me, but I did.

"I'm thinking about renting an apartment of my own, but I need a co-signer. Would you co-sign for me? They said I'm too young, and I have no credit."

"No. I have no credit either. And even if I did, I wouldn't sign my name to it. You don't need an apartment."

I expected that from her. Then I decided to ask Margie's father and grandmother, and they both said they couldn't do it either. They both had cars, so their credit must have been bad, because they didn't give me a reason. I couldn't think of anyone else I could go to, one day I was in the furniture store and decided to explain my problem to Mr. Wilson, who had known me since the first time I went there.

"Mr. Wilson, how you doing?"

"Mr. Evans, how you doing? I noticed that you came in last week and made a large payment. Sorry I missed you. I had gone to a funeral that day. What are you here for today? Have you decided to take delivery of your furniture?"

"I need some help. I'm trying to get an apartment, and I have a job, but they're telling me I need either a co-signer or good credit to get it."

"You can use us as a reference. You have damned good credit here."

"Really, I didn't know that."

"Take my card, and go back there and tell them to call me."

"Thanks."

I went back to the rental office and spoke to the man behind the desk.

"I would like you to reconsider my application and use this as a reference."

I handed him the card Mr. Wilson had given me.

"We'll let you know in a few days."

"Thank you."

Two days later I was in the area and decided to stop by the rental office.

"Good afternoon. My name is Mr. Evans. I stopped by to find out if y'all have made a decision about the apartment I want to rent."

"Good afternoon, Mr. Evans. We were hoping you would stop by. Your application was approved yesterday. The people at the furniture store spoke very highly of you. Today is the nineteenth. How soon would you like to move in?"

"I could move in today if it's okay with you."

"Well, I'll tell you what I can do. I'll give you the keys now, and you can move in when you want. Your first month's rent and your security deposit will be due on the first of next month."

"Okay. I can pay it now if you'd like."

"You can wait until next month."

"I'll pay it now and save myself a trip."

"That's fine with me."

As I walked down those stairs and exited the building, I was overcome with joy. I was so happy and anxious to get home — my *new* home. I ran to catch the bus and thought about staying there that night. No more hanging out in the streets, no more sleeping in the woods, and I wouldn't have to deal with Nora and her crew anymore. I could fix up my apartment the way I wanted it.

On the bus, I lay back and took a nap. When I got off the bus I went straight to the apartment and looked it over thoroughly. As I did this, images formed in my mind of what I would have to do to it and what it was going to look like when I finished, but I didn't tell anybody what I had in mind.

The next day I called the employment office for the Prince George's County school system and learned that I had been hired. I went there and talked to the man who was doing the hiring. "Do you have night work?"

"Sure, we have several night shift openings. Night shift pays more, you know."

"I didn't know that. I would like to work the night shift."

"You got it. It pays about $2.10 an hour. You'll get paid every other week. How soon can you start?"

"I can start next week."

"Okay, you're being assigned to Greenbelt Junior High School. It's on Greenbelt Road, just off of Kenilworth Avenue. Do you know where that is?"

"I sure do."

"You're to report for work next Monday afternoon at 3:30. You'll work Monday through Friday, from 3:30 p.m. to 12:30 a.m. And you're eligible for overtime. That pays time and a half."

I quit my job with the D.C. school system that very day.

Before moving the furniture into the apartment, I gave it a thorough cleaning and fixed it up. I borrowed one of the buffing machines from work and used it to strip the wax from the wood floors. Then I removed all the old paint from the baseboards and sanded them. Finally, I applied a light sealer to the floors and baseboards.

I painted everything except the bathroom and the ceiling. They were okay. I left them white. The walls in the living room I painted rust gold and brown, in a diamond-shaped (12' × 9') pattern. I wanted to match the furniture, which was kind of a rust color with some gold in it. It looked nice. The kitchen and dining area were off- white, the bedroom light blue. The rest I trimmed in white.

Altogether, I spent four days working on it. It wasn't easy, but I enjoyed fixing it the way I wanted it. I didn't leave the apartment except to go to work.

Now it was time to have the furniture delivered. When the delivery truck arrived, I was not only excited but also curious as to how everything was going to look and whether I would like it.

I had bought contemporary furniture: a sofa bed and a pair of matching chairs, a high back, and a low back. I had also gotten two end tables and a coffee table that were made of mahogany.

For lighting, I bought table lamps containing three medium-size globes mounted at the ends of gold rods that were attached to the center of the base. I had gotten those on special order, at $230 each. They too were made of mahogany. The overhead light was a full-size globe with a long gold chain that hung from the ceiling in the center of the living room.

Then there was my stereo component set, with casing and trimming made of mahogany. I also had three large tropical plants, a 25-inch floor-model television set, a bar with four stools, and three large wall pictures.

The dining table was round and white and had matching chairs with blue and white fabric. The bedroom set was made of cherry and consisted of a full-size bed and two dressers. I also had a small television set and a stand for it.

After all the furniture was delivered, I put my receipts into one of the dresser drawers. I had a balance of about $34.00. Then I assembled the bed, lay down on it, and gazed at the ceiling. I was overcome with joy. I thought to myself, I have my own place now and a real bed.

Then I realized that I didn't yet have sheets and pillows for the bed, curtains for the windows, items for the kitchen (dishes, pots and pans, silverware, and other utensils), or towels and washcloths for the bathroom. I didn't even have a wastebasket.

I got up off the bed in a hurry, thinking of all the things I still needed to get.

I finished assembling the furniture, and then I gathered up all the trash and took it out. Finally, I arranged the furniture and swept the floor.

Margie and I were married on the 19th of October, 1968. A justice of the peace officiated. I had just turned nineteen.

When we got back to her house after the ceremony I said, "Start packing. We're moving. I got us an apartment." Her eyes got big. She was so excited.

"Can I see it?"

"Yeah, come on."

We had Barbara watch the baby. As we were walking to our new apartment, Margie's curiosity got the better of her.

"How did you get it?"

"I told you everything was going to be okay."

She smiled and gave me a kiss.

"Who co-signed for you?"

"Nobody."

"But you said *somebody* had to co-sign for you."

"I was able to get it on my own. I have furniture too."

"You have furniture? Where did you get that?"

"I got it at the furniture store. You'll see."

I handed her a pair of keys.

"This key is to the apartment, and this one is to the mailbox. Our apartment is upstairs and to the right. Go on up and take a look at it."

She walked up the stairs, put the key in the door, and looked down at me.

"Come on."

"Go on in. I'm coming."

She walked in and just stood there, totally in awe of what she was seeing.

"Well, do you like it?"

"Yes, I love it!"

She walked around, admiring everything.

"Is all this ours?"

"Yeah baby, it's all ours and everything is paid for. Go look in the bedroom."

She went into the bedroom.

"I like this! Come in here."

When I went in, she was lying down on the bed, reaching out for me.

"I love you. I love you so much. I'm very happy!"

"I love you too."

I got on top of her, and we started kissing — and breathing harder and harder. We started taking off our clothes and kissing each other all over, and then we made wild, passionate love.

Afterward we lay there holding each other.

"How did you get all this furniture?"

"I put it on layaway some time ago. Do you like it?"

"Yes, I love it! I love everything. This stuff wasn't cheap."

"No, it wasn't. I spent a lot of money on it. I got what I liked. I didn't want the same old stuff everybody else had. How do you like the component set?"

"I like it. You'll have to show me how to operate it."

"I will, but first you'll have to go shopping to buy linens, dishes, pots and pans, utensils, food, curtains, and drinking glasses."

I thought to myself, I'm so glad I'll no longer have to drink out of mayonnaise jars or jelly jars.

We got up, washed ourselves off, and put our clothes on.

"Here's $400. Make a list of all the things we need, and ask your grandmother to take you shopping and help you pick them out."

"I want you to go with me."

"I don't need to go with you for that. Just stay away from the cheap stuff. Don't get any curtains for the living room. I think gold drapes would look better in there."

"Yeah, that would look nice."

"I plan to go to J. C. Penney to get those."

"Okay. I have to get back to the baby."

"Wait. I'll walk you back. It's just about time for me to go to work."

I walked her back to her father's house, changed the baby's diaper, and played with him for a while. Then I gave Margie a kiss and left.

Within two weeks we had moved all of her things into the apartment, and everything was pretty much in place. We always had plenty of food on hand. I didn't want my wife and son having to want for anything.

Margie's family came over to see the apartment, and they were impressed. Her grandma would frequently be spending the night at our place so she wouldn't have to drive the 20 miles to get to hers when the weather was bad. Margie's father came over quite often too, mainly to impress his girlfriends.

Even Nora came for a visit. She knew I had moved, and I invited her over a number of times, but a full three months went by before she showed up. When she did, Joe came with her.

I was in the bedroom when I heard Margie say "Hi! Come on in."

"Hi! We were around the corner, so we decided to stop by."

"Make yourself at home. Can I get y'all something to drink?"

"No thanks."

Joe didn't say a word.

"The baby is asleep, but I can wake him up."

"No, don't do that. We're not staying long."

When I came out of the bedroom, Nora and I exchanged hellos but Joe remained silent.

Nora had a devious look on her face, and I could tell that Joe had been drinking. He didn't even look at me. The two of them just stood there, looking around. From the expressions on their faces, I could tell they were stunned, shocked, surprised.

"Well, how do you like it? What do you think?"

"Where did you get this? How did you get it?"

"I worked for it. Not bad, huh?"

She was speechless.

Margie showed her the bedroom while I spoke to Joe.

"Joe, would you like a drink?"

"Nope, I don't need anything more to drink."

"It's okay. I have plenty here."

"I see you do, maybe another time."

Nora came out of the bedroom and walked back into the living room.

"This is nice. Come on, Joe. We have to get home."

"You just got here."

"Yeah, but we have things to do."

"Okay. Thanks for stopping by."

Margie said, "Kenzell has a car. He can take y'all home."

"Yeah, I'll take you home."

I had bought a car, a used one. It was a mid-size sports car, about two years old. They were surprised to learn that I had a car and was driving.

They looked at each other, and then Nora said, "Somebody's waiting for us around the corner."

They got up, and we walked them to the door.

"Good night."

"Good night."

That was their first and last visit.

I knew I had made a good impression on them and that they realized they would never have to worry about me living with them again. Just seeing them had caused me to think of the things they used to say to me.

Jack had already been locked up for the second time, and their other four kids still lived at home with them.

THE FATHER-IN-LAW

I liked my night job, and on Saturdays they taught a course in how to operate blowers, so I signed up for it. At that time the class was full, so I had to get on the waiting list for the next opening. I called every week to find out if anybody had dropped out.

I also started thinking about school again and how I could fit it into my schedule.

I later became night lead man and had two full-time and two part-time employees under me.

I normally got home around 1:15 in the morning, and Margie would have food warmed up for me when I came in. One night I came home and saw that there were more dishes in the rack than usual.

"Why are there so many dishes in the rack? Who has been here?"

"Daddy stopped by with some of his friends, and they had dinner here."

"I see."

On another night I again came home and noticed that there were extra dishes in the rack, and I again asked Margie about it.

"Daddy and his new girlfriend were over."

"I've noticed that he's been spending a lot of time here."

"He borrowed $50. He said he would give it back on Friday."

"Barbara and Willie got married, and they had a baby girl. They staying with his brother and family, who lives somewhere in Southeast, and things ain't going well between them and his brother's wife."

"Why don't they get their own place?"

"I told Barbara that the apartment beneath us is vacant. She asked if you could talk to the resident manager about getting them in there."

"Why you tell her that?"

"She wants to get away from there."

"She should be talking to Willie, not you, that's his responsibility if she don't want to be there."

"I told her that, she said he don't have time to look for an apartment because he's working."

"Alright, I'll call tomorrow morning."

A few days later Margie said, "I was talking to Barbara, and she said that she and the baby hadn't eaten in three days. Can they stay with us until they get the apartment?"

"I don't know if they're going to get it, I did say something to the resident manager."

A few days went by, and Margie again brought up the subject.

"Can we help her out?"

They stayed with us for about two weeks and were approved for the apartment. By the end of the first week I was ready for them to go. They ate everything they could get their hands on and acted as if it was free. The baby didn't get the proper attention and was constantly hollering, crawling around, and getting into everything. She was getting on Junior's nerves too.

I pulled Willie to the side and said, "Hey man, let's walk outside for a minute. I don't mind helping you and your family, but you've got to buy food for y'all. I'm not going to feed y'all too. Y'all been eat everything you see, as if it were free. It's not free to me. I buy food for my family, and I expect you to do the same. It's not my place to provide for you and your family."

"I know man. I've been trying to save money to buy furniture."

"I understand, but you and your wife and daughter got to eat. Furthermore, your daughter has been crawling around and breaking things. She could hurt herself, but neither you nor Barbara says anything to her. She's *your* daughter, it's *our* things she's breaking. You've never offered to replace those things. You can let her do what you want when y'all get your own place, but you've got to put a stop to that as long as you're staying with us."

"Okay man, I'll buy some food, and we'll start watching her more closely, and I'll give you the money for the things she broke."

"Thank you, but don't just buy *some* food. Buy *all* the food your family is going to eat. You know what y'all need and like."

"Do you mind if we stay a few more days, until our furniture is delivered? They said it would be here tomorrow or Thursday."

"Okay."

I just looked at Willie as he walked away. I knew he was upset because of what I had just said. I thought to myself, He has got to be crazy — either that or he's on something. He's been quiet. Perhaps there's something on his mind. He was never like this before. We could always talk, but now he's distancing himself as if he's angry about something. I have no idea what's bothering him, because we hadn't seen each other in a long time prior to his moving in with us.

I could hardly wait for them to go. It was the longest two weeks I had ever lived through.

Once they left I laid down the law to Margie.

"Don't ever ask me to let somebody stay here again."

"Kenzell, I'm just as surprised as you are, and I'm very disappointed in Barbara."

When their furniture arrived, we saw that they had bought a bedroom set and a dinette set that looked just like ours, as well as a sofa and chair that looked like ours except for the color. They wanted to know where we had gotten our lamps and speakers, because they hadn't succeeded in finding anything like them. They were obviously trying to get the very same things that we had.

"Of all the furniture that's available in the stores, they tried to get the same things we have. They should have concentrated on getting the things they really need, so they could stop borrowing from us. I know it's your sister, and I know you want to help her out, but enough is enough."

"Barbara said she told Willie that they couldn't afford that furniture, that he doesn't know how to manage money, and that he should stop trying to keep up with you. She said he then hit her."

"That's not your problem, and you need to stop telling her all of our business."

"I'm not telling her anything."

"Don't give me that crap."

Some time later, I again came home from work and noticed that there were extra dishes in the rack.

"I guess your daddy was here tonight, huh?"

"Yeah, he was here."

"Why does he continue to bring his friends here? And why don't you say something to him about it? He should take them to his house or to a restaurant. I'm not buying food for him and his friends. Shit, I just went through that with your sister and Willie and their daughter, and now I'm going through it with him. On second thought, don't mention it to him. I'll confront him with it when I see him again. Did he give back the $50?"

"Not yet."

"I'm going to say something to him about that too."

I went into the bedroom and turned on the TV. The news was just going off, but I was able to catch the tail end of it, something about a young man by the name of Smelly Williams whose head had been blown off by a shotgun in a robbery.

"I know him."

"Did you say something?"

"No. Perhaps what you heard was the TV."

The next morning Margie said, "Did you see Willie's car?"

"What car? Does Willie have a car?"

"Yeah, it's that brown car parked in front of the building. It's been sitting out there for almost a month now. Barbara said it doesn't run. Willie bought it because *you* have one. She told me not to say anything, because he doesn't want you to know. He doesn't have a license and doesn't know how to drive. It looks as if he's still trying to keep up with you."

"I know Willie's jealous, and I've had the feeling that he's been trying to avoid me. I just pretend not to notice."

One day I heard the mailman downstairs, putting mail in the boxes, so I went down to get our mail. There was the electric bill. I opened it, and it was past due.

I stood there for a few moments, wondering why it hadn't been paid. I kept at least $300 in the dresser drawer for Margie to use to pay the rent and the utility bills and to buy food.

When I went back upstairs, Margie was in the kitchen. I went into the bedroom and opened a dresser drawer where we kept all the bills, receipts, and cash. I saw the electric bill from last month, but no cash! I took the bill out of the drawer and walked into the kitchen.

"Margie, did you pay the electric bill last month?"

"Yeah, I paid it."

"A past-due bill arrived in today's mail."

"That has to be a mistake, because I paid that bill."

"If you had paid it, why are they sending a reminder?"

"I know I paid that bill."

She started getting loud.

"Why are you getting angry?"

"Because you accused me of not paying the bill, and I did pay it."

"Here's the original bill. It was in the dresser drawer, but there's no cash in there. What happened to that?"

"I lent it to Daddy, and he hasn't given it back. I'm sorry."

"What other bills haven't been paid?"

"That's the only one."

"Don't worry about it. I'll take of it."

At that moment something came over me. I felt I couldn't trust her.

"I'll pay the bills from now on."

The feelings I had for her started vanishing and I felt it would never be the same as before.

The next morning I paid the electric bill, and I called the gas company, the insurance man and the rental office to make sure they had been paid what we owed them. They were the only places I needed to call. The furniture and the car were paid for. I still put money in the draw but started paying closer attention to it.

A week later Margie must have noticed I was in a pensive mood.

"What's wrong? Are you still angry with me?"

"No. I've gotten over that. My mind is on something else. I've been talking to a realtor about buying a house, and thinking about trading in my car. I've been looking at a Buick Electra 225."

"When were you going to tell me?"

"I wanted to surprise you."

"Can I see the house and the car you're talking about?"

"Not yet. I still want to surprise you."

I had been thinking about getting a house and trading in my car, but my feelings for Margie were evaporating fast. The thought of her giving my hard earned money, the money I worked for to her father behind my back was something hard for me to comprehend. And I'm doing everything I could to build a better life for us. This was no different from what Nora was doing. I had worked hard to get what I had, and I had considered her to be a responsible person, but this caused me to think otherwise.

As time went on, Willie and I grew further apart. We very seldom saw each other.

About a year later Margie passed on something she had been told.

"Barbara called and said that Willie has lost his job. He's telling everybody he's been sick and is on sick leave, and he wants her to say the same thing."

"I think you should stay out of their business."

"I'm not in getting in their business. She called and told me that."

"Barbara had been covering up for him from the beginning and telling you that she and the baby hadn't had anything to eat. Do you remember how they were sponging off of us when we let them stay here, until I said something?"

"I remember. He wasn't going to work half the time then."

"Well, that's your sister. You knew she was lying all along and making excuses for him. He's lying to her, and she's lying to everybody else. Well, it doesn't matter to me. I ain't got nothing to do with it, and I don't want to hear any more about them, and you need to leave it alone too."

"I haven't been going down there. Barbara's been calling me."

"Listen, my name isn't Booboo the Fool. That's all you talk about. You never tell me about yourself or what you've been doing. I've noticed that for some time now."

I decided to take off from work one Friday because I had taken my car in for service and they weren't going to finish it in time for me to go to work. I called my supervisor to tell him what had happened and let him know I wouldn't be in.

Then I went to the pool hall. Ron was there. He too had taken the day off. I stayed there until around 6 p.m. and then headed for home. When I got there I saw Margie's father's car. The first thing that came to mind was the money he owed us.

When I entered the apartment, Margie and her father looked surprised and were speechless.

"Y'all looking as if you've seen a ghost."

"I thought you were at work."

"What's happening Kenzell?"

"I've been waiting and hoping to catch up with you. I've noticed you been coming here only when I'm not home. I don't want you coming here eating up my food anymore, and I don't want you bringing your friends here to eat and entertain. Take them to your own house. I'm not working to impress you or your friends."

"Also you've been borrowing money from Margie and haven't paid it back. That's my money. She may be your daughter, but she had no business lending you money and you know that. That's money that I saved to pay my bills and support my family. It's been over a month, and you haven't given back a dime of it. I want my $300."

"I'm going to pay you back."

"I want you out of my house right now."

Margie didn't say a word.

"Okay, I'm leaving, but this is my daughter's home too."

"If she wants to go with you, she can, but you're getting your ass out of here right now."

"Kenzell, you don't have to act like that."

"You don't tell *me* how to act. *You* don't pay any bills here. I told you to leave."

"Why, you …," he said in a threatening voice. "You'd better ..."

"Nigger, you don't scare me."

I walked back to the bedroom.

"Daddy, just leave."

When I came out of the bedroom, I had my gun in my hand. On seeing the gun, he started toward the door.

"I'll see you, baby."

I walked to the door and closed it behind him.

"I don't want him here anymore. If he had meant any good, he would have given that money back. He thinks that because he's your daddy he can do whatever he wants. Well, those days are over."

"That's how Daddy is."

I didn't respond to that, because I had a feeling that something was going on between the two of them. Furthermore, I knew I wasn't going to get my money back. Margie's father was the type of guy who needed every dime he could get to keep up his image as a playboy.

For several months I neither saw him nor heard his name mentioned. He still hadn't paid back any of the money.

THE ARREST

I pulled up in front of our apartment building after work one night in January of 1971, at about 1:10 a.m., I noticed that there was a police cruiser in the neighborhood, with two white police officers in it. They were driving slowly, as if they were looking for something. Out of curiosity, I sat in my car for a few moments. While I was there, they came up from behind me and shone a light, first on the building, then on the tags on my car, and finally in my face as they drove alone side of me. Then they drove off.

I got out of the car and started walking toward the apartment. I noticed that all the lights in Willie's apartment were out, as if nobody was there. That's odd, I thought. When I got upstairs, Margie was about half asleep.

"When I pulled up, the police were out here. They shone a light at the building, at my car, and in my face."

"Somebody was shooting out there. The woman who lives in the apartment behind ours called the police. She had been in the bathroom washing up when a bullet shattered her window and landed in her ceiling."

"Did they find out who did it?"

"Somebody said it was a drive-by shooting."

Just then I heard a noise coming from downstairs.

"When I came in, all the lights were off downstairs, as if nobody was home at Willie and Barbara's apartment. Now there's a lot of noise down there, and people are running in and out. Something is going on down there."

"About four or five guys have been staying there."

"You've got to be kidding!"

"I'm not kidding. One of them drives a green car."

A few days later I was coming out of the apartment to go to work. As I approached my car, two white police officers pulled up and got out of their cruiser.

"We want to ask you some questions about a robbery."

"I don't know anything about a robbery. You're talking to the wrong person."

"Let's go inside and talk."

"I'm on my way to work."

"This will take only a few minutes."

"All right."

We went into the apartment, and they started looking around. They didn't say what they were looking for.

"What are you looking for? Why are you going through my apartment? Do you have a search warrant?"

"Shut up. Where did you get this furniture?"

"I bought it."

"You're a damned liar. You stole it, didn't you?"

Margie shouted, "Nothing in here is stolen!"

One of them came out of the bedroom with my gun in his hand.

"You are under arrest."

"What are you arresting me for?"

"Yeah, what are you arresting him for?"

"We want to ask him some questions."

"Do you have a warrant?"

"We don't need one. Let's go."

As we were leaving, Margie hollered, "Leave my husband alone!"

I was taken downtown to Police Headquarters. One of the officers questioned me about a robbery.

"Who are the two guys that were with you in the kidnapping and robbery?"

"I don't know what you're talking about."

"Where were you on the evening of January 4?"

"I was at work. You can check it out with my employer."

"You're a damned liar. Don't you love your family? Don't you want to go home to your wife and son?"

"Yeah, and I want to go home now."

"Then tell me who your friends are."

"I don't know what you're talking about."

He led me to the Sex Squad office, where another officer had some drawings. That officer looked first at me and then at his associates.

"How does this look? Do you think this will do?"

"It will do fine."

"What are you talking about?"

"It's none of your business."

Then he took two or three pictures of me and asked me some questions.

"Where were you on January 4?"

"I was at work. Why?"

"Do you have any cuts or scars on your face?"

"No. Do you see any on my face?"

A few moments later I asked, "Can I make a telephone call?"

"No, not right now, I'll let you make it later."

"I want to make it now."

"Oh, you want to be smart? No, you can't make a call. Now describe yourself."

They asked me how tall I was, how much I weighed, and a number of other questions. Then I was taken to the D.C. Jail and was told I would be going to court in the morning.

The next day I was transported to the courthouse, where the Judge dropped the charges on the grounds that the government had no witnesses and no evidence.

As I was walking out the court room and into the hallway, the U.S. Marshall approached me and said, "I have orders to retain you."

"What orders?"

"They're preparing the papers now."

I was taken back into custody and transported back to the jail and was told I would go back to court in the morning.

The following morning I was transported back to court in front of a U.S. Magistrate.

The government said, "We have a drawing, a description of Mr. Evans in a matter on the date of January 4, 1971, and would like to put him in a line-up."

I tried to say something to the Judge about my whereabouts on January 4, but I was not allowed to speak.

"You will be appointed an attorney," said the Judge.

"I don't see that you have a positive description of him," said the Judge. "Are you sure?"

"We are, and we want to put him in a line-up."

The Judge directed them to place me in a police line-up and said I was to be brought back before him in a week.

I still hadn't had a chance to speak and I really wasn't that concerned since I knew I was at work on the evening of January 4th. I just knew that they would let me go and the description they had of me showed no resemblance.

At any rate, I was taken back to the jail, I saw Willie.

"What are you here for?"

"I was arrested for rape and kidnapping. I have to appear in a police line-up."

"So do I."

As it turned out, Willie and I were put in the same line-up, along with eleven other guys. I was number 6, and Willie was number 13.

"Number 13 is a special case," hollered out by one the detectives in the room of the line-up.

I was picked out and so was Willie. He appeared to be just as incredulous as I was. On our way back to the jail we tried to figure out what was going on. I wasn't worried about it because I knew I was at work on this date.

On February 16, a week after I had appeared in the line-up, I was taken back to court. At this hearing I was informed of a charge pending against me.

"Your Honor, I was at work on that day, and I haven't talked to anybody."

The Judge directed a question to my court-appointed attorney.

"Was the line-up conducted in a fair and meaningful manner?"

"I cannot confirm, since I was not present."

"I don't see that there has been a positive identification. Therefore, I'm reducing bail from $25,000 to $5,000. And I'm not sure that the charge can be submitted to the federal grand jury without a positive identification."

The next court date was set for February 26. I saw no point in trying to make bail, since I had to be back in court in ten days.

LOCKUP

On February 25, 1971, the day before our scheduled hearing, Willie and I were transported to the U.S. District Court in Baltimore, MD., where we were taken straight to the courtroom and brought before The Honorable Judge Leibenlot.

"The grand jury has found a true bill in this matter. You have been indicted on four counts: kidnapping; rape; assault with intent to rape; and aiding and abetting."

We were given a statement of the complaint.

"Bail is set at $25,000 for each of you".

"Counsel will be appointed and will go to the City Jail to speak with you shortly."

We never had a chance to speak.

We were taken to the Baltimore City Jail and placed in a cellblock separate from the rest of the jail. It had two floors and housed only federal prisoners. There were 60 to 70 inmates on the block.

About two or three weeks later, separate court-appointed attorneys visited Willie and me at the jail. My attorney introduced himself.

"My name is Robert Shoemaker. I use to be a prosecutor. I am here to represent you."

"What am I doing here? I was scheduled to return to court in D.C."

"The case was transferred to Maryland."

"I wasn't told that."

"Don't worry about that. It isn't important. I can beat this case for $2,500."

"I ain't got no money, and I have nothing to do with this crime. I was at work when it took place. I was the night lead man where I worked. There are two full-time workers with the same hours as mine, 3:30 p.m. to 12:30 a.m., and two part-time workers who come in at 7:30. I had the keys to the building, and I had to be there to open the doors for both groups of workers. You can check it out.

"Would you be willing to take a lie detector test to prove your innocence?"

"Yeah, I'm willing to take any kind of test they got."

"I'll check that out. Give me the names, addresses, and phone numbers of the workers you supervised, if you have them."

"I can give you the name of my supervisor and the address of where I worked and he can give you all the information on the employees who worked there that evening. Also, the description they have of the perpetrator doesn't fit me. They should be looking for somebody with cuts, scars, and blemishes on his face and straightened hair. As you can see, I don't have any cuts, scars or blemishes on my face, and I my hair been like this all my life."

"I'll get back to you soon."

He left, and I returned to the cellblock. Willie had already returned.

"What did your attorney say?"

"Nothing really, If I give him $2,500, he can beat the case."

"My attorney introduced himself and asked me where I was on the fourth of January. I told him I don't remember. I asked why we're being kept here. He said the case has been transferred here and that he'll have to prepare a defense and start making preparations for the trial."

I met quite a few guys at the jail, most from Baltimore or Maryland county and Washington, D.C., including some from other parts of the country. Most of them were bank robbers, drug dealers, or drug users, though some were there for other crimes. I think Willie and I were the only two who were there for rape.

Visiting hours were 9 a.m. to 3 p.m. every day.

One day my name was called over the intercom at about 2:35. I rushed down the hall to the visiting room, not knowing who had come to see me and realizing that there wouldn't be much time for a visit. When I got there I saw that it was Margie. It was my first time seeing her since my arrest. I hadn't heard from her either and it had been over two months.

The visiting room was long and narrow, about 9' × 30', with thick glass running down the center from one end to the other, to prevent any physical contact. The inmates sat on one side and the visitors on the other.

There were chairs lined up on both sides, facing the glass, and there were telephones mounted next to them so the inmates could chat with their visitors.

"Hi."

"Hi. Where have you been? Where's Junior?"

"He's home."

"I tried calling you every chance I got, but I got no answer. Where have you been? Why I haven't heard from you?"

"I heard you were here, but I didn't know how to find this place and I had no way to get here. I asked Freddie to bring me."

"Where were you while I was at the D.C. Jail?"

"I did go over there, but it was too late. They had already transferred you here to Baltimore."

"Who is Freddie?"

"He's a guy who lives in the neighborhood."

"Why didn't you ask Ron? His number is on the refrigerator door. He and I are good friends. I know I can depend on him. Give him my address and ask him to write me."

"I did ask Ron, but he was always busy. Freddie is the only other person I know that has a car."

"Your father has a car, and so does your grandmother."

"I asked them, but they said they couldn't bring me."

I was starting to pick up bad vibes and felt suspicious about her story — she had always been a poor liar — regardless, I thought I could depend on her, to some degree, especially at times like this. I knew something wasn't right about her story but it wasn't important, and it wasn't the time to think about that.

"There was over $250 in the top drawer of the dresser. You could have used some of that to get here."

"I used it to give Freddie money for gas to bring me here."

"Margie, it doesn't take $250 worth of gas to get from D.C. to Baltimore. More like $5. Why didn't you come to see me at the jail?"

"I was sick."

"Why didn't you bring Junior with you today?"

"He wasn't feeling well, so I left him with Barbara."

"What's wrong with him?"

"He has a bad cold. He'll be all right."

I thought to myself, she must really think I'm stupid now, and feel she can say anything because I'm behind bars.

"I need a lawyer. I need a lawyer real bad. They're pending a rape charge on me. I was at work when this was supposed to have happened. I need you to get me a lawyer as soon as you can. You can ask your grandmother to help you. I'll see that she gets reimbursed."

"Pick up my check at the school, and take the money out the credit union and get me a lawyer. I need one now. There should be enough to hold you and Junior over for a couple months until I get out of here."

The officer in the visiting room hollered, "Visiting is now over."

"I love you."

"You take care."

As she was leaving I thought to myself, I won't be seeing her here again.

When I came out of the visiting room, another inmate name Tony was right behind me. We walked back to the cellblock together. I had met him shortly after I arrived. Everybody on the block knew a little about my case.

Tony was an older Caucasian man. I guess he was in his late 40s or early 50s. He was a big man about 210 pounds or so, a little on the heavy side, soft spoken, real cool, and quiet. He had a full head of black wavy hair. He was the kind of guy you could talk to, someone who made sense. He had a certain charisma about himself and give the impression that he didn't have a care in the world. But I could tell that something was bothering him, because he paced the floor a lot.

"Kenzell, you were called to the visiting room rather late in the day."

"Yeah, that was my wife."

"That's good. How are you coming with your case?"

"Not so well. I feel as if I'm dreaming and can't wake up. I can't believe this is happening."

"They're some dirty MFs. They don't care. You have to write to organizations such as the ACLU and the NAACP and try to get them involved. Write to your congressman and senator, they're full of it too. But write to them and anyone else you can think of."

"I don't know where to start."

"There are a few guys on the block that can help you write letters."

"I hope so. I don't know anything about writing to a judge or the court or people like that. I have a hard enough time trying to write a regular letter."

"I'll ask them when we get back."

"Thanks, this is all new to me. My head is about to burst. They said

I raped somebody. That would have been the least thing on my mind. I haven't raped anybody, and I don't know a thing about the crime.

"I told my court-appointed attorney yesterday that I was at work when this supposed to have happened, that they had the wrong person. The said he can beat it for $2,500, and I said I don't have any money, then he asked me would I be willing to take a lie detector test to prove my innocence and I told him yeah, I'd take any kinda test they got."

"What did he say to that?"

"He didn't seem to care to listen to what I had to say."

"They don't care. They go along with the government. You need a lawyer."

"I can't believe this is happening. I can't think straight. Nothing about this makes any sense to me, and now my wife is acting weird and I don't think I can count on her to get me one."

"Try not to worry about her now. This isn't the time or the place to deal with it. What you need to do now is keep a cool head and concentrate on getting out of here. Otherwise, it will drive you crazy."

"I'm not worried about her. It's my son that I'm concerned about. But you're right. I need to be trying to get some help."

I didn't want Tony to think I was weak, but I was concerned about my son as well as what was happening to me because I strongly believed in the justice system. I definitely didn't think I would be going through anything like this.

"I can't ask my mother, because I know she doesn't care. The only person I have to rely on is my wife and I think she's gone."

"I understand," said Tony, leaning his head to the side and moving his hands as if he was trying to express something. "Let's not talk about that. Just concentrate on getting some help and getting out of here. If that doesn't kill you, it will make you stronger."

I felt he was trying to tell me something for my own good but I didn't want him into my personal business.

When we got back to the cellblock, he introduced me to two inmates I hadn't seen before. They were standing there talking when we walked up.

"Hi! Did I catch y'all at a bad time?"

"No, Tony. What's up?"

"I want y'all to meet Kenzell Evans."

"Hey man, how is it going?"

"How y'all doing?"

"Kenzell, I'd like you to meet Bill Dulles, he's a member of the Black Panthers, and this is John Lee. He's a jail-lawyer. I told Kenzell I knew somebody who might be able to help him. The government is screwing him."

The two of them said simultaneously, "We *have* heard."

"What have you heard?"

"Tell us what we don't know."

After Tony told them everything he knew about my case, they were very willing to help me. They were quickly able to determine that I knew nothing about law or the ramifications of the law, and that the government was framing me for something I didn't do.

Dulles said, "No problem, Tony."

They wrote letters to several entities in an effort to get me some help: the ACLU, the NAACP, and newspapers, as well as senators, congressmen, and a lot of other people. This made me realize just how little I knew, especially about legal matters. I had always thought I was rather hip, but now I realized that I wasn't hip at all, just an ignorant somebody who felt helpless in the face of what was happening to me.

Everybody who replied to those letters gave me the same line or close to it: The judicial system works like this, and this, and that. Nobody helped me.

Dulles said, "Welcome to the system."

A few days later I learned that Tony wasn't white. He was ethnic Italian. I had never known the difference. In my world everybody was either black or white.

Tony shared his cell with another Italian guy. They played gin rummy a lot. Tony's involvement with others in the jail was limited, and he never had much to say, but for some reason he did talk to me.

In fact, everybody took to me, and I got along with all of them. Regardless of my problems, I talked to everybody.

One day Lee said, "You know, Tony really took a liking to you. He carries a lot of weight out on the street as well as in here. A lot of guys want to get close to him. You may have noticed that he doesn't eat the same food that we do. His food comes in from the outside. He can get anything in here, too."

"Why can't he get out?"

"Ask him."

A couple months went by with no word from Margie. I wrote her two or three letters a week and got no response. I called, and nobody answered

75

the phone. One day there was a recorded message to the effect that the phone had been disconnected, so I gave up.

I had a feeling that Willie knew something but he wasn't telling me, and he and Barbara had been communicating and he was hiding her letters from me. I never questioned him about anything, however, since he and I hadn't been close in quite some time. Although he and I were involved in the same case and were in the same cellblock, I had an alibi and he didn't. He was riding on my coat tail.

I figured that Margie was running around on me, but I didn't care. My feelings for her had long gone, but I needed her to get me a lawyer. It never occurred to me that she would turn her back on me at a time like this. Maybe her father has something to do with it.

The most important thing right now was getting a lawyer and getting out of here.

I felt that the reason why Willie kept everything to himself was that he thought it would hurt me to know what was going on.

As time went on I started going through some changes. I felt as if I was in a bad dream and was unable to wake up. I just couldn't believe what was happening. It was hard to accept the fact that it was real, that I had been charged with rape of all things. I felt like I was the victim.

All sorts of thoughts were going through my head as I attempted to figure out who was playing this game with me and why. I was beginning to think I would never get to go home again, that I was being railroaded. I was pretty much out of it, depressed, down in the dumps, helpless, and weak, with very little drive to do anything. I felt as if somebody had blown a hole through me. I felt hollow inside because of being locked up on a charge I knew nothing about. It took so much out of me. I was hurt. I felt stripped of my dignity and character.

I worried so much that the hair on the top of my head had started thinning out and a bald spot was developing there. I started going to the inside hospital sick line for medication, saying that my nerves was bad, I was given Valium, Thorazine, and anything else I could get to take my mind off my problems. The whole business was driving me crazy. I had never felt this bad before. I didn't say much to anybody during this period. I kept to myself.

My court-appointed attorney returned to see me.

"I checked out your witnesses, and they don't work there anymore."

"How can that be? Are you sure you went to the place where I worked?"

Now I was again confronted with survival. This time I was fighting for my freedom, my life, and my son. I still had the desire to make something of myself and to make a way for him.

Meantime, I started adapting to my environment.

This time my court-appointed attorney was accompanied by the U.S. Attorney.

"I want to prove to the U.S. Attorney that you have no scars, cuts, or identifying marks on your face. You won't be allowed to speak while he's examining you."

The U.S. Attorney walked over, looked at me, and then walked away.

"The U.S. Attorney wants to know if you would cop to five years with an A2 number."

"No, I won't. And what happened to the witnesses at my place of work?"

"I told you they're no longer there, but don't worry about that. I'll get back to you in a short while."

"What about the possibility of holding separate trials?"

"No."

I knew I needed help, but I didn't know who to turn to. One day I had a chance to make a phone call and I called the place where I had worked, but they didn't accept long distance calls. Then I wrote to them and my letters was returned, my mind was never clear about that. It left me wondering why.

I could think of any one else in particular to call. As a last resort, I called Nora's place. Patrice answered the phone.

"Hello."

"Hi Patrice"

"Hi, Barney, someone told me that Margie has been giving away your furniture. I couldn't believe it. I heard she was moving to somewhere in Maryland. Can I have some of your things?"

"I don't care. I'll talk to you later."

SHORTY BIG SHOES

That night Willie and I were in our cell playing cards when the lights went out. We knew that the night officer always locked the cell doors and made a count of the inmates at 10 p.m., and shortly thereafter some of the lights would be turned off. That night I noticed that certain doors and the TV room had been reopened after the count was over.

"Do you hear that noise downstairs?"

"That's from the guys who clean up."

"They always clean up before 10:00, but it's already later than that and at least five of the cell doors are open. The guys from those cells will be out until midnight, when the officer gets off. Either one of them knows him or he's being paid off. They don't eat jail food either. They have their own food and a little stove to cook it on. They're selling bacon and eggs and steak sandwiches for money or cigarettes, and they watch TV until midnight."

"They have it made."

"The drug boys get out and spend most of their time playing poker for money, cigarettes, and commissary items. They welcome anybody who wants to play. This may be a way for me to get out, because I know how to play poker — and from watching them, I wasn't impressed."

The games were held in Mac's cell. Mac was a tall, slim guy in his 30s. He was in here for bank robbery.

"Can I get into the game?"

"Sure. You have to have some money, cigarettes, or commissary items. Let me know, and I'll have the officer pop your door."

"How many cartons do I need?"

"About four or five, but that's up to you."

I had some money on me when I was arrested, and I'd been buying commissary items and sharing them with Willie. I went to the commissary and got four cartons of cigarettes.

"I'm ready."

"Okay, I got you."

That evening our door was popped open early and I walked down the to Mac's cell.

"May I come in?"

"Yeah, come on in."

I sat down, and Mac introduced me to the other three guys. We were counted while I was in his cell. All of them were older than I, but that didn't bother me. I played with them for about an hour and a half, at which point they quit because I was on a roll and they saw that everything was going my way.

I ended up with eight cartons of cigarettes, a bag of commissary items, and $530 in cash.

"Are you coming back tomorrow?"

"Yeah, I'll be here."

"You were lucky tonight."

"I'll be that way tomorrow."

I went back to my cell and told Willie how it had gone.

"You won all that?"

"Yeah, help yourself."

"Are you going to quit?"

"No. Why should I quit? I'm in their pocket. Besides, two of them owe me $50. I bet this door will open early tomorrow."

"Man, I think you should quit while you're ahead."

"Willie, I'm not interested in just winning their money. I want the cell door opened. It makes me feel important, just like them. Besides, this ordeal isn't going to last much longer."

This also kept my mind occupied. By now everybody knew who I was. When I wasn't playing cards I hung out downstairs with the other guys, eating steak sandwiches and chilling out, or chatting with Tony. He was more interesting to talk to, and made more sense to me than the other guys.

"How you doing, Kenzell?"

"I'm okay."

"That's good. I see you're getting around."

"Yeah a little, I decided to take your advice. Thanks."

"It's okay. I can only imagine what's going through your head. You know, I gave my wife the world. I was good to her. She didn't want for anything. She left our five-month-old son in the house alone and went out with Jackie Gleason, the actor.

"I could deal with her leaving me, but to leave our son! I was so angry! I got somebody to watch the baby, and then I got my gun and went out to kill them both. When I pulled up to Gleason's house, they were driving off, but I didn't know it was they until I knocked on the door and was told that they had just left.

"After I cooled down I realized that she wasn't worth it. About two months later Gleason dumped her."

I knew who Jackie Gleason was, but I wasn't that impressed with him, I was learning more about Tony without even asking.

"You know, that was a lesson for me. Anyway, you'll more than likely be going up to Lewisburg. I'll be going there pretty soon myself. I have some friends up there that can probably help you. Do you mess with drugs?"

"No. I have experimented with drugs, but that's not for me."

"Good. Leave that stuff alone. It's bad business. Once you're on drugs, you can't get off of them. Whatever you do, stay away from drugs."

"I'm not interested in drugs."

One afternoon about a week or so later, Tony and I were standing around talking when a new inmate came in.

"Tony, I know that guy. I don't know his name, but I remember him from a men's clothing store, Rosenblatt, in downtown D.C. He was the owner. It was my favorite clothing store. They sold the latest styles in brand name clothes, and I could get some good deals there at a good price."

"His name is Michael. I stocked his store."

When Michael came in he walked straight toward us.

"Hi Tony, how are you?"

"Hi Michael, I'm fine. How are you?"

"I'm okay."

"Michael, I want you to meet Kenzell, this is Michael."

"Hi Kenzell, I feel as if I've seen you before."

"It was probably at your clothing store."

"Yeah, that's right."

He broke into a smile.

"I'll talk with you later, Tony."

"Okay."

"Nice meeting you, Michael."

"Same here, I'll see you soon."

As time went on I noticed that Michael did everything Tony told him to do, as *if Michael was a flunky. Some of the guys were saying that Tony was a* Mafia boss, while others thought he was a big dope man, high up in rank.

The dope boys thought they were big, but they were nothing compared to Tony. In fact, they were trying hard to get close to him, going out of their way to be his friend, but Tony wasn't moved by them.

One day the officer stepped inside the block and hollered, "Evans, you have a visitor."

It was 2:35 p.m. I rushed down to the visiting room, not knowing who it was and realizing that I wouldn't have much time with them. To my surprise, it was Nora. My first thought was, I hope she's bringing me some good news, news that she's gotten me a lawyer.

"I was over here visiting my uncle and thought I'd stop by to see how you're doing."

"I'm okay. I still need a lawyer."

"Boy, I ain't got no money for any lawyer, I'm sure everything will work out all right if you pray."

That turned me off.

"I know you're glad I'm out of your way. Don't worry. I'll pray."

She just looked at me.

"And you don't have to come here anymore to see how I'm doing."

As I turned to leave I saw that Tony was in the visiting room talking to three beautiful women. I decided to wait for him in the back. They were nicely dressed and had fur coats on. After visiting hours were over we walked back to the block together.

"They came in from California to see me. In fact, they came from all over to see me."

"They looked like movie stars."

"One of them was."

I thought to myself, who is this guy?

When we got back to the block, Tony went to his cell. I walked to the back, toward a guy by the name of Mark whom I had met and occasionally spoke with.

Mark was a fat black guy from Washington. He loved to talk, and he was a fast talker. He was a little taller than me and weighed about 180 pounds. He wasn't really fat. He just looked that way, I guess because he was big boned.

He was about three or four years older than me and seemed to know a little about everything and everybody. He acted as if he was right at home and didn't let anything bother him. He'd say what was on his mind and let it go at that. Mark was a bank robber, and he admitted robbing banks for a living.

"Hey, Evans, what's up?"

"Hey Mark!"

"I see you had a visitor."

"Yeah, it was my mother."

"Yeah, that's who visits: mothers and lovers, and a friend now and then."

"Don't you get visits?"

"Nope, my mother died when I was very young, and I never met my father. I'm not married. There are some girls that I used to flirt with, but they weren't mine. They were there for any guy who wanted them. I didn't want to waste my time getting caught up in that. I've been in and out of jails most of my life.

"When I first got locked up it was for stealing and hitting a man in the head. He was trying to protect someone else's merchandise as if it belonged to him, that stupid MF! I was only nine years old at the time.

"Man, I'm a bank robber, and I will rob a bank again if I got the chance, but I wouldn't take an amateur with me again, like that co-defendant of mine. He can't even follow instructions. That's why we got caught, a stupid MF! I've robbed plenty of banks by myself and succeeded in getting away. I found him in the gutter begging every time I saw him, and I tried to help him make something of himself. I should have left his ass there. You live and learn."

"Man, you're crazy!" I chuckled. "You shouldn't talk about your co-defendant like that."

Mark's co-defendant's name was Jim Black. He was a black guy, twenty-one years old, 5'8", about 160 pounds. He liked playing cards with his friends and cracking jokes. The 15 years he'd just received didn't seem to faze him.

"Jim is just like *your* co-defendant: retarded. I think there's something about Willie that isn't quite right, but I can't seem to put my finger on it. You probably can't see it, because you have a lot on your mind right now."

Directing my attention to the guys on the top tier, Mark said, "See those guys up there? They're amateurs. They want to be seen as bank robbers, but all they do is whine and complain. They can do the crime, but they don't want to do the time. You'll see what I mean as time goes on."

Mark and I became pretty good friends.

"You know, the U.S. marshals don't tell you when they're coming. They just show up unexpectedly and sweep you up. I know I'm going to Lewisburg, and I can't wait. When you get there, you've got to get to the library and learn some law. They railroaded you, man."

"Yeah, I know. I try not to think about it, because it upsets me and I have no clue how it happened. In fact, it hurts me."

"I'm sure it does, but don't give up. When you get there you'll have a chance to get some real help."

"I'm not trying to go to Lewisburg."

"Well, that's where you'll end up if they don't release you. You can fight it and make your life more miserable then what it is or you can learn the system and deal with it. Once you get to Lewisburg, you'll be able to make life a lot easier on yourself. Just don't get too comfortable.

"As for me, I have a 15-year sentence to serve there, and I plan to enjoy myself while I'm there. I can't wait.

"Just remember this: When you're busy enjoying yourself, time moves along a lot faster. You're doing the time and not letting time do you. You see a lot of these guys have it all wrong. I'm a veteran at this, you know. A lot of these guys don't know how to do time. You'll see."

As time went on I watched them come and go. One day a guy from Baltimore named George Lewis came in. He was a drug dealer. He knew the guys from Baltimore, but didn't know me and wanted to meet me because they knew me, so he came up and introduced himself in his own unique way.

"Where did you get those brogans—those shoes you're wearing?"

"These aren't brogans. Where I come from, they're called hustling shoes."

"Those are brogans. Do you like wearing those big things?"

"Big? What are you talking about?"

George started calling me Shorty Big Shoes, and somehow that name stuck. Everybody called me Shorty Big Shoes after that. They never knew my real name, and that was fine with me.

DOUBLE LIFE PLUS 15

Our trial commenced at 10 a.m. on Monday, June 7, 1971. Willie and I had a white Judge, a white prosecutor, all white jurors, and our white court-appointed attorneys. Everyone but Willie and me was white.

The Judge ordered the media out of the courtroom, and the doors were closed.

With the media out I felt that it was my last chance for hope. I wanted the media there for everyone to see how I was being railroaded.

"Why aren't the media allowed in?" I asked my attorney.

"Don't worry about that. It's not important. Just be cool."

"Why are there no blacks on the jury?"

"We couldn't get any blacks, but the government is offering us a plea bargain. Would you plead to ten years with an A2 number?"

"No. I'm not pleading guilty to anything. I don't know a thing about this crime that I've been charged with. And what do you mean, you couldn't get any blacks? There are plenty of blacks who live in the Baltimore area, but all of these jurors are old white people. And they weren't selected by the normal process. They just came in and sat down."

"We will object to that."

There were no witnesses and no evidence against us. All they had were some stipulations that the attorneys had agreed upon, based on just a handful of documents: the police report; the victim's description; the FBI report of Special Agent H.B. Ray's investigation, to the effect that the victim was picked up in Washington, D.C., and subsequently transported first to Virginia and then to a federal reservation in Fort Foote, Prince George's County, in the State and District of Maryland, was within the territorial jurisdiction of the United States; and the report of the doctor's examination, which took place after the victim arrived at the hospital. All of this was admitted as evidence.

Judge Dan E. Leibenlot presided at the trial.

"For the government: Frank A. Hill.

"For defendant Evans: Robert Shoemaker.

"For defendant Gray: Nate O. Young."

The opening statements, made by Mr. Hill, were brief. They were based on the aforementioned documents.

Mr. Shoemaker called no witnesses on my behalf.

Mr. Young had nothing at all to say.

During direct examination Mr. Hill called his only witness: the victim, Miss Betty Ann Smith. She was a young white woman, twenty-six years old. She was homely looking and was dressed like a Mennonite, definitely out of touch with the times. She looked as if she was there to put on a show, and she did. Mr. Hill coaxed her along. You could see that she was lying, following his lead. The identification of the perpetrator was never established, though Willie and I were pointed out but, she couldn't even look at us. The only thing she managed to do was point her finger in our direction.

When Willie and I got back to the jail, Tony and Mark asked us about it.

"How did it go? Was everything all right?"

"They already had a jury, and there were no blacks."

"There were no blacks on the jury?"

"No, and I asked my lawyer about that. He objected to it, but his objection was overruled."

"Still, you should have had at least one black juror."

"I didn't know that, but I did ask about it and I was told there was nothing wrong with the jury."

"Well, you have grounds for appeal. I bet the jury was made up of a bunch of old white people."

"That's exactly what it was, and the Judge sent the media reps out of the courtroom and closed the doors. Everybody was white — everybody, that is, but Willie and me."

Just before the trial resumed, my lawyer came over and spoke to me.

"The government is offering you five years. You'll be out in no time."

"You don't understand. I'm not pleading guilty to something that I know nothing about. I've never seen that woman before in my life."

"Well, suit yourself. I couldn't get in touch with your witnesses."

"What do you mean? I'm sure they still work there."

"No, none of them works there anymore, but we do have an expert witness, a guy who straightens hair. He'll explain to the jury how he can tell that you could never have had your hair straightened."

"I don't need a witness like that. The description of the perpetrator doesn't fit me. The person they're looking for is tall, and I'm short. He has scars, cuts, and blemishes on his face, and straightened hair. I have no marks on my face. Anybody can see that. Moreover, I don't have straightened hair. Why wasn't this brought out? They haven't established a positive identification."

He didn't say another word. I thought to myself, if I were white, would it have been different?

At 10:00 a.m. on June 8 the trial resumed. The attorneys picked up where they had left off the previous day. Everything was essentially the same: direct examination followed by cross examination. At 4:30 p.m. the court was adjourned until the next morning, Wednesday the ninth.

When Willie and I got back to the City Jail, the other guys again questioned us.

"How did it go?"

"It was the same as yesterday."

On Wednesday the attorneys went back and forth to the bench and finished up with the presentation of the closing arguments. At 4:50 p.m. the court was adjourned until Thursday morning.

On Thursday, June 10 the court reiterated the charges and read the instructions to the jury. At 10:30 a. m., the jury began deliberations. They came back within an hour and rendered a verdict of guilty.

We went back to the jail, speechless. I was so hurt. I just couldn't believe it. I didn't think that what was happening to me was real. George and some of the other guys tried to lift our spirits.

"Don't give up. You have to keep on fighting."

"Did they offer you any kind of plea?"

"Yeah, they offered me ten years. Later, they offered me five years with an A2 number."

"Really, what did you say to that?"

"I refused, I didn't commit the crime. I wouldn't feel right admitting to something that I know nothing about. I'm innocent."

"I understand."

As Willie and I waited in the City Jail for sentencing, some of the guys were sitting around talking trash and carrying on. One of them, a guy by the name of Mitchell Green, was waiting to be transferred.

"Shorty Big Shoes, when you go up for sentencing and the Judge asks you if you have anything to say, answer him by saying 'Yes, your Honor. Don't hurt me. Help me. Be gentle with me.'"

"What?"

"I robbed a bank and pleaded guilty. I was going to cop a plea to 15 years when I went up for sentencing. The Judge said, 'Mr. Green, do you have anything to say before I pronounce sentencing?' 'Yes your Honor,' I replied. 'What is it?' he asked. 'I love my family, and I want to get a job when I get out.' The Judge said, 'Okay. Is there anything else you want to say?' 'Yes your Honor, My wife just gave birth to our daughter, and I would like to be home with her, with both of them.' The Judge said, 'Okay, anything else?' 'Yes sir. Don't hurt me. Help me.' The Judge said, 'Okay. Is there anything more?' 'No your Honor, that's about it.' The Judge said, 'Okay Mr. Green, I'm sentencing you to 25 years in the federal penitentiary under the U.S. Attorney's Office.' '25 years! I can't do 25 years! That's a long time.' The Judge said, 'Mr. Green, just do the best you can, and don't worry about the rest.' 'Okay your Honor.'"

In September of 1971 Willie and I returned to court for sentencing.

"Kenzell Evans and Willie Gray, I am about to pronounce sentencing. Do you have anything you wish to say, Mr. Evans?"

"I did not commit this crime, Your Honor. I was at work at the time it occurred. That woman may have been raped, but I didn't rape her."

"Is there anything else?"

"No."

The Judge turned his attention to Willie.

"Mr. Gray, do you have anything you wish to say?"

"I have no alibi. I don't recall where I was on that day. Your Honor, I didn't commit this crime."

"Mr. Gray, is there anything else you wish to say?"

"No sir."

"I am sentencing you, Kenzell Evans and Willie Gray, to two life sentences each, plus 15 years to be served concurrently at the U.S. Penitentiary in Lewisburg, PA., under the U.S. Attorney's Office."

I thought to myself, this man has got to be crazy. How did he fix his mouth to say that?

Margie and Barbara did show up for a few days during trial and again on the date of sentencing. This time she had Junior with her. Barbara was there too, with her daughter. Margie said to me, "That woman was lying, and they knew it. They knew you weren't the perpetrator. You were framed."

I didn't say a word. I was too hurt — and too upset — to speak. I felt like I had been branded.

When the marshals arrived to take us back to the courthouse cellblock, Junior yelled out, "Leave my daddy alone! I want my daddy!"

As I turned around to say something to him, the marshals pulled me away saying, "You can't talk to him."

Again Junior screamed, "Leave my daddy alone!"

I'll never forget that look on his face. It was as if he knew what was going on and had gone into shock. That image of him has stayed in my mind, and that was the last time seeing Margie and Junior.

The marshals took us back to the City Jail.

"We will be picking you up shortly and transferring you to Lewisburg."

During that same week the marshals came and picked up Michael, Tony and a few others. Before Tony left he asked me, "Do you need anything?" Then he handed me a bag that contained soap, toothpaste, and a number of commissary items and added, "I'll see you in Lewisburg."

"Thanks."

It seemed that most of the guys from the cellblock were leaving or gone or sent to Lewisburg to serve their time. Mac, Jim, and Mark had left two weeks earlier. Before departing, Mark had said to me, "I'll see you when you get there, partner."

Now that Mac was gone and the dope boys were gone the gambling was over and we were back in our cells. The officer did pop the cell doors a few times and let us out to watch TV for a little while since he knew me.

JIMMY HOFFA, FRIEND

As a rule we weren't told when or where we were going after sentencing, unless it was to another court appearance. On October 26, 1971, about a month after sentencing, two marshals showed up and said "Let's go."

We quickly got our things together and were ready to go.

While we were packing, a few guys came by begging for soap, toothpaste, and whatever they could get, trying to convince us we wouldn't need these items where we were going. They maintained that we would get everything we needed when we got to Lewisburg.

Willie kept all of his belongings, but I didn't want to carry mine. It was nothing but junk to me. I ended up giving most of my things away, but I held on to all my legal documents.

After the farewells we were taken downstairs, where the marshals were waiting for us with chains in their hands. They took our belongings and put them in the car, and then came back and put handcuffs and leg shackles on us. We were put in the back seat, and the marshals got up front. Then we pulled away.

"Where are we going?"

"You are going straight to the federal penitentiary — unless you make an attempt to escape, you would save us a trip."

When we left the city limits and drove out onto the highway, I sat back and started to observe the scenery as I asked myself, what is this, modern slavery? Is this really happening to me? I was taken from my home, from my family against my will, jailed, framed, railroaded, and branded for life.

How many others have this been done to? Because I was one of those people who strongly believed in the system, but the system proved me wrong, it damn near blow me out of my mind. So never say it won't happen to you.

I thought about my Mama who had raised me. Why did she die and leave me like this? I thought about aunts, uncles, and cousins of mine whom I hadn't seen in a long time, and wondered whether they knew about what I was going through. There was no point in thinking about Nora and Joe and their other kids, because they didn't care — except when there was something they wanted from me.

I didn't want to waste my time thinking about them. Maybe they were right when they said I would never amount to anything.

At least I don't have to worry about hearing that anymore.

Margie had disappointed me. I realized that I didn't know her after all. It had been only my feelings, and not hers, that were involved in our marriage. I hoped my son be okay. I missed him.

Who was she, this rape victim? Why did she get on the stand and lie? I had never seen that woman in my life, and she had never seen me either. She couldn't look at me when she was on the stand. I knew she was lying, and so could everybody else in the courtroom.

Maybe somebody paid her to say what she did. I don't believe she was ever raped. She was homely looking, and she wore a country-looking dress and a pair of old eyeglasses that looked as if they could have belonged to her grandmother. Somebody had probably told her to dress like that, to get sympathy from the jury, because people didn't dress like that anymore.

I still had no idea what had become of the guys who had worked at the school with me and why my phone call was not accepted and why my letter returned. My attorney said they no longer worked there and couldn't be found. None of that made any sense to me.

My thoughts were suddenly interrupted when one of the marshals spoke.

"We are almost there."

I sat up straight and tried to get a better view. Before I knew it they had turned off the highway onto a long road lined with trees on both sides. As they drove up that road, a long tall gray cement wall came into view, behind it stood a large, castle-like structure.

I noticed that the parking lot was full of cars and the surrounding grounds had been kept up quite well.

The marshals drove up to the tall steel gates and displayed some papers to the guard.

"We are bringing in two prisoners."

I was a bit curious. I had never been in a penitentiary before, though I had heard a lot about them. For that matter I had never had shackles on before, and I had no idea what to expect.

The marshals took us inside to Receiving and Discharge (R & D), where they turned us over to the prison warden and removed the shackles and handcuffs. They brought in our belongings and turned them over to the R & D officer, and then they left.

"Take off all your clothes and put them on the table. Now what do you want us to do with them? Send them home, throw them into the trash, or donate them? You won't need them here."

Willie said, "Send my clothes home."

I thought about this for a moment and realized that I had no home to send anything to.

"You can donate mine or throw them in the trash."

Another officer came over and directed us to the showers.

When we got out he issued a series of orders in rapid-fire succession.

"Spread your legs, hold up your balls, open your mouth, stick out your tongue, turn your head to the right and the left, pull your ears forward, run your fingers through the hair on your head, and put your hands out in front of you and turn them over. Now turn around, bend over and spread your cheeks, show the bottoms of your feet, and step to the side."

Then we were given new clothes: three pairs of underwear, three T-shirts, three pairs of socks, three shirts, three pairs of pants, a pair of shoes, a pair of boots, and a belt.

We were also given a toothbrush and toothpaste, two bars of soap, a comb, three washcloths, and three bath towels. The kind you get in a hotel. We received a razor and razor blades, plus a can of shaving cream or shaving powder.

"You should always have a clean shave, with no mustache. You'll dress properly at all times, with your shirt tucked into your pants and your shoestrings tied. And always wear a belt."

The inmates were dressed as though they were in the military. The officers wore gray uniforms with light-blue or gray slacks and a dark-blue blazer.

"An inmate from the barber shop will be coming to get you."

As he was telling us this, the inmate walked in.

"Are they ready to get their hair cut?"

"We're done with you. You will follow him to the barber shop."

After our hair was cut off and shaved, we were taken to the Admission & Orientation dormitory. All inmates go there when they first arrive, for ten days.

During the first two days we were given a physical examination. Then we were sent to the education department for testing. We attended orientation meetings nearly every day, where members of the staff came in and told us what was expected of us and what was prohibited. We were told that breakfast was served from 6:15 to 7:25 a.m., lunch from 10:30 a.m. to 12:20 p.m., and dinner from 4:30 to 5:40 p.m.

Then we were taken on a sightseeing tour of the institution, which had a capacity of about 1,100. The population was about 80 percent white and a few from other countries. Most of the blacks were from Washington, D.C. The rest were mainly from the East Coast, with just a few from other parts of the U.S. The food at Lewisburg was good, and it was run like a military installation.

I saw a few guys from the neighborhood I lived in, guys I knew from the street. We exchanged only a few words: "What are you here for? How much time did you get? Have you seen so-and-so?" Those were the most common questions asked when inmates arrived, especially the one about the amount of time, which was something that applied to everybody there and provided a natural way to categorize inmates. I started seeing more guys I knew, a few of whom I had met at the City Jail.

The library was large. It had every major newspaper and magazine from all over the country and some foreign newspapers. Everything was up to date, although a few of the publications were a day or two old because of the distance involved in shipping them here. They had books covering everything, including some *How to Do It Yourself* books. The legal section had all the latest law books and received all the latest decisions. There were approximately a dozen typewriters for inmates to use while in the library, and six portable ones that could be checked out for use in the cells. Stationery and postage were free, and several inmates were available to provide assistance.

After touring the library, we toured the hospital and the education department, and were told we would tour the other departments after lunch.

We were taken to the cafeteria (or "mess hall," as they called it) to eat, and we were told to report back to A & O after lunch, for further orientation sessions.

Willie and I and a few other guys were going through the cafeteria line when somebody hollered out, "Damn! There's Shorty Big Shoes! Shorty Big Shoes is here!"

I looked up and saw Mark. With a half-smile on my face I nodded and said, "Don't do that."

"Man, fuck them! I don't give a shit about them!"

He was excited to see me, and was loud about it.

"We're going to roll now!"

"I don't know what you're talking about."

In a more subdued tone he said, "We'll talk later." Then he got loud again and yelled, "That's Shorty Big Shoes!"

The inmates stared at me and then looked down at my feet. They probably wondered if I had big feet.

Mark carried on as if I was somebody important.

"I'll see you later."

Actually, that allowed me to loosen up, because I had been a little tense being new there.

I was like a walking time bomb, but I managed to control my emotions and reactions so they wouldn't show. I was a hurt man.

Once we got our food, we sat down at a table. Later, Mark came up to us, pulled up a chair from another table, and sat down. Everybody seemed to know him.

"Hi, Willie," he said, and then he spoke to the other guys at the table. "I can't stay long, because I have to get back to work. I'm a cook on the morning shift. Try to get a job in the kitchen, on the morning shift." Then he stood up.

"Do you have any cigarettes?"

"No."

"Here's half a pack. I'll come up to A & O and bring you some cosmetics, commissary items, and cigarettes. Now I have to get back to work."

Just as Mark was about to depart, Tony walked up.

"Hi Mark."

"Hey Tony, do you see who's here?"

"Yeah, I see him."

"Well, I have to go. I'll talk with y'all later."

"Hi Tony, I was just about to ask about you," I said.

"Hi Kenzell, Willie," Tony said before greeting the other guys at the table.

"Hi."

Tony then directed his attention to me.

"Is there anything you need?"

"No. Mark said he would bring up some things for me."

"Alright, I'm going to let you eat now, because y'all have to get to your next orientation session, I'll be in the yard this evening if you decide to come out or come and see me when you get out of A & O. I'm living in E2 annex, in the back."

"Okay, I will."

I felt much more relaxed after getting the attention from Mark and Tony. Even after they left, the guys were still looking over at me with curiosity.

After we ate we went back to A & O, and had more orientation sessions.

Later that day we had mail call. Willie got a letter. He and Barbara had been writing each other the entire time we were locked up, and he still hadn't said anything to me and I never inquired because I didn't care, it was the last thing on my mind. I just left it alone.

That evening Mark came to A & O and handed me a large bag and a combination lock. Just after I put the bag in my locker, Willie came by.

"Willie, here's the combination to my locker. If you want something, you're welcome to get it."

"All right, thanks."

"Come on, Mark. Let's go out to the yard and talk."

"Have you heard anything from your lawyer regarding your case?"

"No. I haven't heard from anyone."

"Shoes, I can only imagine what you are going through. I am a bank robber, and if I had been framed like you have, I know if it was me, I would be fucked up too, and don't know anything about it, who wouldn't be? It got to be bothering you, but you can't let this get the better of you. You've got to meet with some of these jailhouse lawyers. I personally don't know of any, so you'll need to go to the library.

"This is nothing like the City Jail. It's the real deal here. You have to grow up fast. It's best not to let anybody know your business and stay out of everybody else's business.

"You've got to let go of your mama and daddy, brothers and sisters, wife, son, everybody. You need to concentrate on what's going on in here, not what's happening out on the street. That's something you have no control of. It shouldn't make any difference anyway, you know?

"Besides, you're doing a life sentence. Man, I got 15 years with the federals and 20 years' backup to do in Maryland. I'm not going to sit around here worrying about it the way a lot of these guys are doing."

"I don't expect to stay here for the rest of my life."

"I don't blame you, but as long as you're here you might as well enjoy yourself instead of spending all your time worrying. You should get to know your environment. This is totally different from the jail. Try to get something out of it. And keep in mind that there is no life without hope."

"Have they assigned you to a job yet?"

"Yeah, I'm going to the mill."

"I don't think you're going to like it there, you should consider taking a job in the kitchen, in the mill you'll get about $32 a month. By working in the kitchen you earn about $10 to $15 a month for about one hour a day, five days a week and you can make more money hustling on the side, making and selling sandwiches and wine."

As Mark and I were walking I saw Tony, who called me over to where he was sitting.

"You go on and talk to Tony. I'll catch up with you later."

"All right, Mark."

Mark exchanged greetings with Tony and then left.

"When did you get here?"

"I'm still in A & O. I think I'm coming out tomorrow."

"Oh, there's Jimmy. Do you know Jimmy Hoffa?"

"No, I don't. Who is he?"

"He was once president of the Teamsters Union."

Tony called him over.

"Hi Tony, It's a beautiful day."

"Yes it is. Listen, Jimmy, I'd like you to do me a favor."

"What is it, Tony?"

"I want you to meet Kenzell."

"Hi, Kenzell, how you?"

"Kenzell, this is Jimmy."

"Hi, Jimmy."

"The government screwed him. They railroaded him. He's really in need of help. Do you know anybody that can help him?"

"Yeah, I'll introduce him to a friend of mind. Kenzell, I have another mile to go. Why don't you come and walk with me while we talk? We might run into him on the way."

"All right, thanks Tony, I'll see you around."

While we were walking, Jimmy asked, "What kind of case is it?"

"It's a rape and kidnapping case and I know nothing about it."

"I'm asking only so I'll be able to pass it on to my friend in case we don't see him now. By the way, I work in the laundry room on the presser. If you bring your clothes down there, I'll press them for you."

"All right, I'll do that."

As we walked around the track for the second time, he saw his friend sitting on a bench, reading a newspaper. We walked over to him.

"He might be able to help you. He spends a lot of time in the legal section of the library. He was a spy from Russia. He's been here for over 17 years, trying to get back to his country."

"Russia?"

It freaked me out when he said Russia.

"Yes Russia. Hey, Naberezhnyi, how you doing?"

I couldn't pronounce or remember his name, because it was long and looked so different from American names. He was a big man, about 6'3", 230 pounds. He had a head full of white hair and looked to be in his mid 50s.

"Hello, Jimmy, how you doing? It's a beautiful day, isn't it? I came out here to get a tan."

"It sure is. I had to come out and get some exercise. I want you to meet Kenzell."

"Hi! Are you enjoying this beautiful day?"

"Hi. I sure am."

"He needs some legal help. Do you have time?"

"Sure, I can help him."

He turned to me and said, "I can help you if you're ready and willing to help yourself."

"I'm ready and willing."

"Do you know anything about the law?"

"No, I don't."

"Meet me in the library around 7:00 tomorrow evening."

"I'll be there."

Jimmy thanked him and said, "I'll see you guys around. I have a few more laps to go."

"I'll see you around, Jimmy."

"Thanks again for the help, Jimmy."

"Think nothing of it. I'll see you later."

I directed my attention to the Russian.

"I'll let you go back to reading your book and getting your tan, and I'll see you tomorrow evening."

"Okay, I'll see you tomorrow."

I left and started walking around the track, thinking about what Mark had said, and then I went back inside.

I still didn't know who Jimmy Hoffa was. When I saw Mark again I asked him.

"Who is Jimmy Hoffa?"

"He's a big union man, president of the Teamsters."

"He didn't look big to me. In fact, he's not big at all."

"He may not be big physically, but he's big. He stopped all the union trucks from running. He and Robert Kennedy didn't like each other at all."

"Why?"

"Kennedy thought Hoffa was backed by the underworld, the Mafia, and he tried to break it up. Why do you ask?"

"Tony introduced me to him."

"Oh yeah, Tony's a heavyweight. He's in the family, the Mafia family. He's got a lot of pull."

"He does?"

"Yeah, I got the scoop on everybody, and I know everything that's going on around here. Shit, you're lucky that Tony took an interest in you back at the jail. When you get a chance, you've got to go to E2 annex and see how they live back there. He runs this place, man."

The following evening I went to the library to meet with the spy. When I walked in he was seated at a table with about six books opened up. He was reading one of them. I walked over to the table.

"How you doing?"

"I'm doing fine. Pull up a chair and sit down. You don't know anything about law or filing of court documents?"

"No, I'm afraid I don't."

"There's a book I want you to order. The title of it is *Wigmore on Evidence*. Be sure to read it."

"Here's all the information you need to order the book."

"I'll do that. Thank you."

Once all the orientation meetings were completed Willie and I moved out of A & O. Willie was assigned to "C" block on the second floor, and I was assigned to "A" block on the third floor. Both of us were assigned to work in the mill, in the sheet metal department, where we helped make lockers, bookcases, and file cabinets for all the government agencies. In the other part of the factory they made clothing: pants, shirts, and coats.

After spending two weeks there, I could tell that that kind of work wasn't for me, so I asked for a transfer to the kitchen. Willie stayed there. I got a job in the kitchen, but not on the same shift as Mark.

A couple of days later I took my clothes down to Jimmy for pressing. I did that only one or two more times. After that I just sent my clothes to the laundry. That was good enough for me.

The first chance I got I wrote to the Lewisburg Prison Project, the Prison Research Council at the University of Pennsylvania Law School, Howard University, American University, Walter Fauntroy (non-voting delegate to the U.S. House of Representatives for the District of Columbia), and several other sources of possible legal assistance, but I got no help from any of them.

When the book arrived, I read it and then got back with the Russian.

"I can teach you all I know, but you'll have to use your own wits to take you further than that, if you know what I mean."

"I understand."

He showed me how to research cases, how to write notes about them, and how to file motions with the courts.

One day I received a copy of a motion on false identification from my court-appointed attorney, together with a letter saying that he had filed it with the Court of Appeals on my behalf.

I showed the motion to the spy. He read it and said, "Your attorney didn't do a good job on this. The false identification was a good issue, an important one, and it could have gotten you back in court, but now it's too late for that."

"Why?"

"You get only one shot at it, so you have to get it right the first time. He really didn't say anything relevant. He ruined that for you."

"I see."

HUSTLING

I was working in the afternoon, on the second shift. One day I was sitting at one of the tables and thinking about home when Mark appeared out of nowhere.

"What's happening?"

"Not a thing."

"How long have you been working in here?"

"I just started a couple of days ago. I had to get out of that mill. It reminded me of my job on the outside. I tried so hard to do the right thing there and look where it got me. They took that from me and ruined my life and now they want to put me in the mill working for them. Damn that mill, I got out of there. Besides, that job in the mill was so dirty."

"How about if we hook up together, you and me?"

"What do you have in mind, Mark?"

"We can make money on sandwiches by selling them in the evening. An egg salad sandwich would sell for one pack of cigarettes. Roast beef and all the other meats would sell for two packs. We could also make wine. I can show you how to make it. A small trash can holds five gallons. We could sell a pint jar of wine for five packs of cigarettes and a quart jar for ten, and we could get 25 packs for a gallon. We could sell the cigarettes for cash, at $10 for five cartons."

I appreciated Mark friendship, because I didn't know a thing about the penitentiary. He had taken the time to be my friend when he didn't have to. I guess getting me involved in these activities was his way of helping me take my mind off my situation.

"The two of us would make a good team."

"Why didn't you get Jim to work with you? He's your rap partner."

"Shoes, I wasn't lying when I told you I found him in the gutter. I tried to help the boy, but he's a hopeless case. Believe me, he is. And Willie's just like him in some ways: sorry, lazy, and slow. But that's something you'll have to see for yourself. I don't know Willie that well, but you may have noticed that the guys at the City Jail didn't have much to say to him. You're still young, and you have a lot to learn.

"You and I can turn the cigarettes into cash, and use the cash to get some work done on your case."

"Alright, but I don't want any shit out of you. It has to be a 50/50 partnership."

"It's a deal."

We had our hands in everything. We were on a roll. However, Mark would lose his cigarettes and money as fast as he earned them. He had a bad gambling habit, but he didn't care. "Easy come, easy go. I make money. Money didn't make me," he would say.

I was doing all right for myself. Everybody knew who I was, but I knew most of them only on a surface level, which was fine with me. A lot of guys were coming to me to pawn their watches or borrow cigarettes, so I decided to open up some stores and pawnshops in the dorms and cellblocks, some on each end of the penitentiary. I handpicked guys to manage them.

Prison rules allowed inmates to have only four cartons of cigarettes at any given time. Anything over that was considered contraband. I had well over 200 cartons of cigarettes at a time, spread out over a number of cellblocks, on every floor of many of the dorms. Most of the action was in the dorms. I paid $10 a month to nonsmokers to hold my cigarettes, and I took care of the smokers' habits as long as they held three cartons of cigarettes for me.

About a month or two later I got a letter from my attorney.

The Appeals Court denied the motion. I'm in the process of pursuing it all the way to the Supreme Court.

I showed it to the spy.

"I would get rid of him."

I took his advice.

Please take the necessary steps to dismiss yourself from my case. Also, please send me a copy of my transcript and all the papers pertaining to my case.

Thank you.

When I saw Willie I filled him in on what had transpired.

"I received a letter from my attorney saying that the appeal was denied. I wrote back and asked him to send me all my papers."

"I got a letter from my attorney too, and I'm going to write him back."

The next time I saw the spy it was in the mess hall. I went over and sat down at his table.

"How you doing Evans? I haven't seen you in the library lately."

"Yeah, I know. It's been hard trying to keep my mind focused right now. I dismissed my lawyer and requested that he send me a copy of my transcript and all the other documents pertaining to my case, and he did. After reading through everything, I discovered new evidence. The police report, the investigating officers, and the warrant were all fabricated. Furthermore, they bore no signatures.

And on top of that, we were never taken back to court in D.C. on February 26 for the preliminary hearing because they didn't have a positive identification and enough proof and felt it would likely have been dismissed. Instead, we were taken straight to Maryland and indicted."

"Evans, he was a court-appointed attorney. He didn't care about you. He wasn't doing you any good."

"According to the report of the FBI investigation, they did go to my place of employment and interviewed my witness, pubic hairs were taken from the victim immediately after the crime, and pubic hairs were taken from Willie as well, together with rags they said had been used. Microscopic analysis failed to reflect any hairs of Negroid origin among the pubic hairs of the victim. Also, the blood and semen stains tested negative. The victim also had a twin sister who lived the street life, but none of this was presented in court."

"I would like to read what you have."

"Okay, I told him I had been at work when the crime supposedly took place and four employees were working there too. I told my attorney and he came back and said he couldn't find any of them and that they didn't work there anymore, but they entered my supervisor's name in the transcript as a witness. Keep in mind that the only two witnesses who actually testified at the trial were the victim and a guy who does hair."

"Well, it's a good thing you dismissed your attorney. I can only imagine how you feel, especially after finding this out."

"I was never comfortable with him from the beginning, when he said he could beat this case if I gave him some money. He asked me for money more than once."

"I'll need about three or four days to read everything."

"Okay."

I went and got all my material and gave it to him.

"All right, I'll get back to you in a few days."

A week later I saw the spy again.

"I read everything, and I see what you're talking about: The government had a weak case, and they definitely covered the evidence up to get a conviction. Then they covered their tracks. Your attorney knew that the motion on identification wasn't going anywhere, before he even filed it. That was discussed at the bench in the presence of the Judge.

"They were working together. Only two witnesses were called at the trial, but ten witnesses were listed in the transcript as having given testimony. How could that be?

"There are a lot of wrongs in your case: motions that your attorney prepared and didn't file, and an important motion that he filed and later withdrew. Your attorney is definitely incompetent. You should prepare a motion against him. You definitely have enough ammunition. There have been a lot of cases dealing with incompetent attorneys. You need to get back into the library and research those cases, but be sure to take your time and do it right."

I was sitting outside on a bench one day and started to reflect on my experiences. Before coming to Lewisburg, I had never been in the presence of so many white guys. Virtually everyone in my past had been black. I wondered where I had gotten the idea that all whites looked alike, because I now knew that that's not true. They're different in many ways, just as blacks are.

At Lewisburg there were people from all over the United States and a number of foreign countries. I began to recognize differences, in behavior and background, between the Italians, the Jews, and people of other nationalities and ethnic groups. Maybe that's what Mark had been trying to get me to do: open my eyes.

I looked up and realized that the yard was closing. I got up and started walking rapidly toward the door.

It was about four or five months later that I saw the spy again. I had been drifting away from my research. He kept busy and was always focused on what he was doing. He made it seem easy, and he was on top of everything he did. I wish he could have done the research for me, because he was far more knowledgeable than me and he made it look easy.

One day he said to me, "If you want it done, you'd better get started.

I noticed you don't have the same drive and energy you had when you arrived here. What's wrong? You weren't expecting me to do it for you, were you?"

"In a way I was hoping you would, because you're more knowledgeable and you make it look easy, but I couldn't ask you to do it. I'm still hurting from that horrible ordeal. Thinking about it makes it hard for me to concentrate. I haven't forgotten what you showed me and told me, and I appreciate it, but I have a lot on my mind. I guess being in here for something I didn't do—especially rape—is pretty hard for me to come to grips with. But I know I got to get myself together and work on my case."

"I understand what you're going through, and you have a right to feel the way you do. They robbed you of your freedom, but you've got to break loose and work on it. No matter how hard it is, you got to break loose. Where there's a will, there's a way.

"I can show you what to do, and that's what I have been doing. If I did it for you, you would know something about it but you wouldn't understand it. It doesn't matter how long it takes. As long as you're going up to that law library you'll eventually achieve your goal, but you need to have a good understanding of what you're dealing with before you go into battle. You know what you have to do, but be sure to take your time and do it right.

"I've been here for nearly 18 years, trying to get back to my homeland. I've long since gotten beyond the stage of sitting around and thinking about how your government has treated me. I went through the same thing you're going through. I had to go into that library and teach myself. I've filed over ten motions, and they were all denied. This time I believe I'll win this battle. I've been waiting for 28 months for the court to make a decision."

Two weeks later I went to the library looking for him. He wasn't there, so I asked one of the law clerks if he had seen him.

"The hack (the officer) came to his cell the other morning and told him to get all of his belongings and report to R & D immediately. He was sent back to Russia."

"I know he's happy."

"Yeah, I'm sure he is."

WILLIE

I can't recall how many times Mark and I were locked up for taking food out of the kitchen. I'd been caught with cases of eggs, bread, mayonnaise, onions, steaks, grapefruit, tomato paste, yeast, and sugar. We took only the things we needed to make our sandwiches and our wine. The administration called it stealing. I didn't care.

No sooner than I get out I went right back into hustling. That was my way of adjusting to penitentiary life. I was learning everything about the penitentiary, inside and out, and I learned it fast.

I didn't work on my case during the day, because I was too caught up in penitentiary life. When I did give it some attention it was at night, when I was alone in my cell.

On one of the occasions when I was locked up and charged with making and distributing wine, I was given five days in "the hole" (solitary confinement). Being in the hole never bothered me. In fact, it was fine with me, because it was a place where I could get some rest.

I was released late on a Friday evening and returned to the general population. Before I could get my things unpacked, a guy from Ohio walked up to me.

"You'd better go see about your rap partner. He's at the movies."

"What do you mean, go see about him?"

"He'd been drinking wine with those guys from D.C., and he was arguing with a guy from Baltimore."

"Thanks."

I left my things in the cell and went up to the movie theater to look for Willie. When I arrived there I was unable to find him, but I did see a

106

few guys from Baltimore and D.C. congregating in the hall. Most of them had gotten drunk on wine. I went over to them.

"Have you seen Willie? What's going on?"

"I don't know. I just got here, but I heard that Willie and John got into an argument about that faggot named Frankie. John supposed to be his man, and Willie had disrespected him in front of Frankie by saying things like 'You're a faggot yourself' and 'I should make you my woman.'"

"Willie was drunk and was trying to impress the guys from D.C. He should apologize to John."

John was from Baltimore.

"You're right. Let me go find Willie so I can squash this shit before it gets out of hand."

I walked down the hall and could feel the tension as I went past a few guys from Baltimore who was standing around together. I went to Willie's cellblock and walked up the stairs to his cell, where I found him sleeping. I called out to wake him up.

"Willie, Willie, Willie."

"Yeah"

"What's going on?"

"Nothing is going on."

"Something's going on, because there's a lot of tension out there. What is it between you and this guy named John?"

"Oh, that faggot. Man, he didn't do a thing to defend himself, and those niggers he hangs around with didn't want to fight."

"What are you trying to prove? Who are you trying to impress, those guys? Man, they don't give a damn about you. You've been wasting your time running around with them, drinking wine, and talking about your homey. You should be working on the case instead of fucking with them. I told you running around with them were going lead to this. You'd better wake up."

Willie was into that kind of nonsense, getting drunk and going around with his so-called friends, looking for attention while concealing their fears. I never did care for that.

"Man, you don't understand. I'm okay. I'm not trying to impress anybody."

"Did you squash it?"

"There was nothing to squash. I told you he didn't want to fight. I wish you would stop pressing me about that bullshit."

"Man, You got to wake up."

"I'm okay."

I'll see you in the morning when your head is clear."

The following morning I had to be in the kitchen by 5:30 a.m., and I wasn't able to take my break until around 6:45. When that time came I decided to go and have a talk with Willie, because he hadn't come in for breakfast. As I was walking down the hall toward his cellblock a guy by the name of Ronnie walked up to me and said, "You'd better go see about Willie."

I knew Ronnie from the neighborhood. As he rushed by me I grabbed him by the arm and questioned him in a whispered tone.

"What you talking about?"

"I have to go!"

He was so scared that he wouldn't tell me anything more. Since running wasn't allowed, I walked to Willie's cell as fast as I could. When I got there I saw that there was blood all over the cell walls. I muttered "Damn" and eased back out of the cell. Then I walked down the hall where there were several guys standing around. I saw a guy from D.C. by the name of Marvin. He was a friend of Willie's. They played cards together. I remembered Willie telling me something about he let Marvin use one of his watches. I walked over to him and whispered.

"What happened?"

"I don't know. I had nothing to do with it."

I went on down the hall, thinking to myself, Damn! I thought Marvin was Willie's friend. They played cards, talked, and worked together, but he couldn't or wouldn't tell me what had happened. He too was scared.

I went downstairs and on out of the cellblock. A guy by the name of Paul walked up to me. He had been at the City Jail with us.

"I heard about Willie getting stabbed. Is he all right?"

"I don't know. All I know is that there was blood all over his cell. I don't even know where he is."

"I've got a shank. You need some help?"

"No, I'll be okay. Besides, nobody's talking right now."

Later, Mark came down the hall and said, "I heard Willie got stabbed. Are you okay?"

"I'm fine, but nobody wants to tell me what happened."

"That's because they're all afraid that you'll retaliate. I have two shanks right here, just in case we need them."

"I don't need it."

"You never know in a situation like this."

"Alright, I'll put my left hand behind me, and you can slide it up my sleeve. I got it."

I'll keep it on me, just in case.

Then Tony came down the hall toward me with five of his friends. They were all younger than him. Two of them had razor blades between their fingers. Tony walked up to me and asked,

"Are you okay?"

"I'm fine."

"How is Willie?"

"I don't know. I don't know what happened, and no one will tell me."

"Don't worry. I'll find out for you."

After Tony left, another guy from D.C. approached me. He had bought wine from me many times. His name was Walter. He had been at Lewisburg for about four months. Before that he served 17 years at the penitentiary in Leavenworth, Kansas.

"Hey Shoes, you all right?"

"Yeah, I'm okay."

"I heard what happened. I know you just got here and don't know what's going on. I heard your partner was hanging with the guys from D.C. They aren't worth shit, man. They pretend to be his friends, but they didn't come to his aid. That's how they are. Did you go to the lieutenant's office to check on him?"

"No."

"Well, go and find out what happened to him. They'll tell you, but they won't tell anybody else."

I went into the lieutenant's office.

"Willie has been stabbed eight or nine times, in the chest and arm area, but it isn't serious. He's been taken to a hospital off the penitentiary grounds. The last word we had is that he's going to be okay."

"Thank you."

"Don't go starting up anything, we have everything under control."

"I'm not."

"We found out who did it and why, but you need not concern yourself with that."

As I was leaving the lieutenant's office Tony walked up to me.

"I guess you heard that Willie's going to be all right."

"Yeah, they took him to a hospital on the outside."

"I know. Willie got into a beef with a guy named John from Baltimore about a faggot he's with. Willie had been drinking that homemade wine with some guys from D.C. last night and was threatening John at the movies. John felt he had to do something about it, since so many people had heard Willie. Anyway, there's nothing to worry about now. The faggot knew he couldn't remain in the general population after what had happened, so both he and John checked into the hole."

"I guess I'll have to watch out for John's friends."

"You don't have to worry about them. Besides, most of them like you."

A couple weeks later I found out that a few of the guys who lived on the floor with Willie knew that the stabbing was going to take place even before it happened. One of guys was from D.C. who had given John the shank to use to do it, and they were there and saw it occur, but no one did anything to prevent it. They were his so-called friends from D.C. who played cards and ball with him, but when his life was threatened they turned their heads.

After hearing that, they weren't true friends of Willie's anyway. They were cowards. I stopped speaking to them, and had nothing more to do with them since.

Shortly before the stabbing incident occurred I was moved to B block. I had been put out of the kitchen and given a 20-minute-a-day job as an orderly on the block. Mark was still around, making sure we got everything we needed to keep our business going. I would go down to the kitchen during his shift to help him make up the sandwiches and figure out ways to get them out of the kitchen without getting caught.

One day while I was looking out of my cell window, which faced the windows of the hospital, I saw Willie directly across from me, laughing.

"You okay? I was concerned about you."

"Yeah man. That chump was scared. He was faking."

"Faking? You could've lost your life, man."

"I wasn't worried about him."

"How could you *not* be worried about him, considering that he walked in on you while you were asleep?"

"Oh man, I wasn't dreaming. When I woke up and realized what was happening, he ran."

After hearing that, I thought to myself—he doesn't realize how stupid he sounded. I cut the conversation short.

"Is there anything you need?"

"No."

"Well, I have to go. I'll talk with you later."

I thought perhaps the hacks had moved me to a cell across from Willie's hospital cell to find out if I knew anything about what had happened.

The next day Willie was moved, and later that week he was transferred to Terre Haute, IN.

I told Mark about Willie's transfer when he came down to bring me some sugar for the wine.

"Man, for a short time they had Willie in a hospital cell right across from my cell. He's gone now though. They transferred him to Terre Haute."

"I know. I saw the transfers list."

"Man, you don't know how relieved I am. He was a big liability to me. You just don't know."

"I told you he was just like Jim."

"I see that now. He always wanted to compete with me or challenge me in some way or another, but he ended up being frustrated because I never agreed with him.

"Willie showed no desire to work on our case either. I talked and talked to him about it, and he made several attempts, but he always gave up. He was having too much fun hanging around with his friends."

"I told you. I'm sure the other guys noticed it too. You know what that mean, don't you?"

"What's that?"

"You're growing up."

"Shit."

We laughed.

111

MAYORS AS BUNKMATES

There wasn't a dull moment after Willie was transferred. I felt much better knowing I didn't have to worry about him anymore. I guess it felt like an extra load was lifted. There was always something going on or something to do.

In the meantime, I continued worked on my case and sent him copies of everything I did.

The guys who ran one of the football pools came to me to bail them out. In return they gave me a share in their business plus interest. I ended up taking that over, and now they worked for me, but I continued to let them run everything and I stayed in the background and took a piece of the action every week.

The stores and the pawnshops were doing well. I always kept $700 to $800 in my pocket for gambling and buying contraband from the outside. I didn't use any of it on my case because everything was free.

I was into everything that had something to do with acquiring money — all, that is, except drugs. I was doing so well that I had started smoking cigars.

Right before Christmas in 1973, it was announced that the commissary would be closed for two weeks for inventory. That was fine with me, because it meant that a lot of guys would be coming to me. I knew I was going to clean up.

At that time we were also told not to drink the water, because they found dead bugs in it, perhaps from the spraying of the crops on the other side of the wall during the summer. They weren't sure but were looking into it. In the meantime, drinking water was being boiled in the kitchen and rationed to the prison population, one dorm at a time. We weren't allowed to go into the kitchen until after the water was rationed.

Mark and I couldn't afford to shut down our operation for that two-week period. We had to get our wine made for the holidays.

He said to me, "You know we have a lot of competition out there."

"So? That's always been the case, but we have nothing to worry about. We have lots of customers, and most of them have placed their orders with us."

"We have to figure out a way to get water out of the kitchen."

"I have an idea."

"What is it?"

"We'll get it out of the toilet, and nobody will know."

"How are we going to use it?"

"I'll take care of that. We'll need a 50-pound bag of sugar. I have everything else."

"Fifty pounds, how much wine are you planning on making?"

"We can make 50 gallons. I have two 25-gallon barrels upstairs in the orderly closet. We can fill them with water from the toilet, and I'll take a sheet to cover the barrels. Shit, nobody will know. They'll think we stole the water from the kitchen. Besides, they say alcohol kills germs."

Before we broke it down, Mark went to the hospital and stole two bottles of alcohol.

"Pour one bottle into each barrel, to give it a kick."

We made one barrel with wheat germ and the other with tomato paste.

"Big Shoes, they're going to love this. I told them it would be ready tonight."

It was gone in two hours, and they were bugging us for more. I told Mark, "That went real fast. They loved it and kept coming back for more."

"I wish we had made more. Oh, a hillbilly came to me and said you were supposed to hold a gallon for him. I told him we were sold out. He was a little warm too."

"That isn't what I said. All I told him was when it would be ready. I don't know what makes some of these guys think I'm going to hold it for them. Oh, I did look out for Jay."

"Jay, the Muslim?"

"Yeah, he pulled me aside one day last week and said he isn't supposed to eat pork but he loves pork chops. He said, 'Don't say anything, man, but can I pay you in advance to slip me a couple sandwiches and a jar of wine without anybody's knowing?' I told him I would take care of it for him. He said, 'Thanks, brother.'"

"He does the same thing with me. That's why I always tease him, but I don't share his secret with anyone else. A lot of these guys are like that, but he's all right. Man, I'm going to get into the poker game."

"Okay, I think I'll go see Tony."

"I'll see you in the morning."

Tony's friends in E annex included three mayors: one from Newark, another from Atlantic City, and a third from Trenton. They were on the north side of the penitentiary. All the Italians lived on the north side.

They ate well and always kept plenty of bread sticks, crackers, cookies, Italian sausages, salami, and cheeses on the table, with beverages and stacked too. They had wine and liquor by the case.

I was always in good spirits when I went up to visit Tony.

"Merry Christmas!"

"Merry Christmas, buddy! Get something to eat."

They were always good to me, as if I were one of them. I had met some of them through Tony but had forgotten their names. However, they all knew who I was. One of the guys ran a football pool. He bought most of my cigarettes for the case I got.

Tony said, "How you doing? You okay? Sit down. Do you need anything?"

"No thanks, I'm okay."

"Don't get too comfortable in here. You have to keep working on your case. Don't give up. You've got to get yourself out of here."

"I'm still working on it, mostly late at night when I'm in my cell. I had to put it down for a while because it was getting the better of me. I'm doing what I do to take my mind off of it, but I'm not giving up."

"I understand, but you got to put everything you got into it, or you will end up in here for the rest of your life. We are talking about your freedom. You have to take it seriously and deal with whatever comes with it. You understand?"

"I understand."

"You know, if you can do as well as you're doing for yourself in here, you can do a lot better on the outside. You would do okay in business."

"Tony, I've never thought of that."

"Sure you can. Come on. Whatever you do, don't get involved in drugs." Offering me some food, he said, "Help yourself."

"I'm not really hungry. Besides, I need to be on my way, because it's getting late and I have a few more stops, but I will have a bite."

I had heard that Italians don't like you to turn them down when they offer you something to eat, so I took a few slices of salami and some cheese and crackers.

Tony reached over and pulled a fifth of Scotch out of the case and handed it to me.

"Merry Christmas, Kenzell."

"Thanks Tony, same to you."

I got up and left. On the way out I stopped and chatted with Jim for a while. He lived in E2, in the same building as Tony, but they were in different dormitories. I showed him the bottle of Scotch Tony had given me.

"Damn! He gave you that?"

"Yeah, would you like a drink? Get a couple of cups, and we'll have a drink together."

I sat down.

"You know, the mayor of Trenton sleeps right across from me. Did you see him back there?"

"I saw him."

"He trembles when Tony stops by and tells him to do something. He's always doing a lot of writing too."

"I see you're learning to play chess."

"I'm getting pretty good at it."

I stood up.

"Well, Merry Christmas, Jim. I hope you have a good year ahead and many more to come. Right now I have to go."

"Thanks. Same to you, Shoes."

As I was leaving, I thought about what Mark had said a while back. Jim was nothing like Mark. They had nothing in common. Sort of like Willie and me. Mark was a go-getter who would make things happen and was always on the go, doing something. Jim was more like Willie, except that Jim could read people better and knew how to mingle. He also liked to engage in debates.

Willie didn't know what he was talking about most of the time, but he tried to give his friends the impression that he did. They would look at him as if he was stupid or crazy. Both Jim and Willie were slow and lazy.

I stayed up late that night and wrote to the District Court, requesting a copy of all the proceedings pertaining to my case. I included my case number and the pertinent dates.

I wanted to know why I wasn't returned to court on February 26, 1971, for my scheduled hearing.

A week or so later I got locked up for making and distributing wine again. I had heard that Jimmy Hoffa was released.

When I got out this time, Tony was gone. In fact, a lot of people had left. All of the Italians were gone. I asked Mark, "Where did everybody go?"

He said, "I don't know. They just started leaving. I think it was a political move. I don't know if they have gone home or what. Oh, Tony told me to remind you to get back on your case. I think he went back to court."

"I wish I had seen him before he left. Oh well ..."

The institution was changing, and the population was increasing faster than ever before, with more blacks and fewer whites. Now it was about 80 percent black and 20 percent white, with the number of whites constantly decreasing. The population was up to about 1,400 and growing.

"Do you remember Nick, the guy who used to cut hair in the barber shop?"

"I remember him."

"I read in the paper that he and a few other guys had hooked up with Jimmy Hoffa when they were released and now they're all dead. There were pictures of them being released from Lewisburg."

Hoffa had been set free some time back. President Nixon had granted him clemency.

THE FIGHT

In 1974, I was moved to E1 dormitory, where all the action was. There I could stay up all night gambling or participate in whatever was going on. When I had nothing in particular to do, the guys would gather around my area, eating sandwiches and telling lies.

The dorms weren't the place to be if you had to get up in the morning for work or do some studying. This was definitely a change for me, for I had always been in a cell, where I could get plenty of rest and work on my case if I wanted to.

One day I stole a cow shoulder from the kitchen and took it to the dorm to make steak sandwiches. Everybody was talking about that. I said to Mark, "I've got to get out of this dorm. I'm drawing too much attention to myself. I have no privacy."

"It has drawn a lot of heat."

"I know, and these niggers are worrying the shit out of me. I can't get any rest. They're all nosing into my business, trying to see what I'm doing, and I have to listen to all their problems. Shit, I'm not their damned caseworker."

"When you're doing well, you pick up plenty of friends. You don't have to know them or seek them out. They just find you. I always tell them I'm busy and don't have time."

"I have to get back to the cellblock so I can breathe and function better. They don't need to know everything we're doing, any more than we need to know everything they're up to. Frankly, I don't care what they're doing. Our concern lies solely in meeting their demand for sandwiches and wine and supplying them with cigarettes."

117

"You're right."

"I'm going to ask to be moved today."

"Okay, I'll talk with you tomorrow."

That night I didn't do any gambling. I tried to get some rest instead. There were a few guys in the dorm that I tended to talk to, and they made a habit of bringing their chairs over to my bed area. I enjoyed listening to them at times, telling lies, cracking jokes, and talking shit.

There was a Puerto Rican guy named Ramos. He slept on the top bunk bed, above me. He had just finished playing cards and was upset because he had lost. He got up on his bunk and said, "I'm going to bed."

He turned the light off. I stood up and turned the light back on and said, "I'll turn the light off when we finish. It won't be long."

"They can go somewhere else. I want to get some sleep."

He reached over and turned the light off again.

I got up and turned it back on.

"Hey man, they were here with me before you got here. I'll turn the light out as soon as we finish."

By that time one of the guys sitting around my bed — a guy by the name of Wayne — stood up and said, "Man, what's your problem?"

"Wayne, stay out of it. It doesn't concern you or the rest of y'all."

We sat back down to finish our conversation, and Ramos sat up and turned the light back off. I paused for a moment, thinking to myself, I don't believe he did that. Has he lost his mind?

"Ramos, don't bother the light. We're talking. I'll turn the light off as soon as we all finished our drinks."

I sat back down, and Ramos again sat up and turned the light off.

"Fuck that! Y'all can go somewhere else. I'm going to bed, and I want this light off."

At that moment two thoughts crossed my mind: Is he crazy, or does he think I'm playing with him? I got up and again turned the light back on.

"Please don't touch the light again. I'll turn it off when we finish."

"Fuck that! I'll turn the light off when I please. I'm going to bed. They can go somewhere else."

"You fuck with that light again and I'm going to get in your ass."

As I turned to sit down I noticed Ramos reaching for the light. I hit him in the face as hard as I could and he fell off the top bunk, to the floor. I jumped on top of him and started hitting him in the face.

He started hollering, "Help! help! Somebody help me!"

A few guys pulled me off of him saying, "Stop Shoes! It's not worth it. You're going to kill him."

There was blood all over his face, as he hollered for help.

Someone said, "That's what you get, mother fucker."

When they pulled me off of him, I went and grabbed a mop wringer and swung it back. As it was coming toward Ramos's head one of the guys grabbed it, pulling it from me.

"Shoes, it's not worth it. It's not worth it."

Then I heard another guy speak.

"What he's telling you is right. I know it's the principle of it, but it's not worth it."

Another guy hollered out, "He got what he deserved, stupid mother fucker."

I suddenly realized that I had lost control and was trying to kill him.

Before I could say another word it seemed that everybody was grabbing me and pulling me to the floor, shouting "Get him! Hold him!"

By that time, Ramos had managed to get up and was starting to bang on the dormitory door for the hacks to come and get him out of there. He had blood all over his face. The hacks took him to the hospital.

I knew they would be back to lock me up. I packed up my personal property and got rid of all the contraband and gave everything to Wayne to hold for me, including about $700 in cash. Not long after that about eight or nine hacks rushed in to get me.

"Evans, pack up your belongings and let's go. Who were the other guys that jumped on Ramos?"

"There was nobody else," some one said.

"He said about four guys jumped him."

Somebody from the back hollered out, "Nobody jumped him. He got his ass whipped."

"Let's go."

Someone else hollered out, "Take care, Shoes."

They took me straight to solitary confinement. The hole never bothered me, because I knew that when I was there I could get some rest. What I couldn't understand was why it was called the hole when it was nothing more than a holding cellblock apart from the general population. I knew that name affected some inmates psychologically, but not me.

After Ramos was released from the hospital they put him in the hole for three or four days and released him. They kept me locked up for fifteen days. While I was there I slept, exercised, read a book, thought about my case, slept some more, and exercised.

To my surprise, Ramos came around to the window of my cell and hollered out, "Shoes, I'm sorry for what happened. My caseworker said I'll be going home in ten days. You take care, man."

I was shocked. I didn't say a word. I just pondered on what he said. Why was he telling me this? He should have told that to the committee, the hack he had lied to. If you're man enough to create it, you should be man enough to deal with it. It made me wonder why he would want to make a scene like that, knowing he was due to be released in two weeks. He could have sacrificed his freedom or even lost his life over that light. Maybe he had nowhere to go.

At any rate it gave me something to think about. Here I was, doing two life sentences plus 15 years for a crime I hadn't committed. Being here was like having a license to kill. What could they do if I were to commit a real crime? Give me a third life sentence? This is crazy.

The incident with Ramos had given me an opportunity to release a lot of tension. Once I cooled off I realized that violence is not the way to deal with conflict—and that it wasn't what I wanted. It made me think about what was at stake and what I had almost gotten myself into. I knew I had to change the direction of my life.

Again, I remembered what Mama used to say: *Sticks and stones can break your bones, but words can never hurt you.* I also reminded myself that my son needed to have me in his life, and thought about what tony had said. So I vowed to control my temper and redirect my energy toward meaningful goals, such as getting out of prison. I didn't want to be there for the rest of my life, and I knew I had to make some drastic changes if I was ever going to get out.

A guy from Philadelphia was put in the cell next to mine. I remember seeing him the day he came to Lewisburg. One day he got a Dear John letter from his wife, saying she had found somebody else. He couldn't handle that, and he was very upset and depressed. When the hacks came to feed him, they found him hanging from his bed sheets in his cell.

Damn! I thought, he hadn't been here long, not more than a month or so. He evidently didn't have the fortitude to deal with the situation that had confronted him.

I thought, Here I am, with double life plus 15 for something I didn't do, and I had nearly snuffed out somebody's life over nothing.

I knew that if I were to do anything like that I would end up being in prison forever.

They brought Ronnie in and put him in a cell across the hall from mine. He was that scared guy who had told me to go see about Willie when he got stabbed. On that occasion he had begged the hack for a Bible. He didn't know I was there, and when he got back into the general population he pretended to be a hard-nosed guy. I didn't say a thing. I had seen a lot of that: pretending. Riding the fence, as some called it.

We received mail even while we were in the hole. I got a letter from the District Court while I was there.

Unfortunately, we have no records or documents pertaining to your case number from the period of time you indicated.

I thought, they have got to have a record of my being there. Otherwise, how could I have been transferred from Washington to Baltimore? They had essentially kidnapped us and must have destroyed the documents.

I wrote them a second letter.

I appeared in the District Court in Baltimore on February 25, 1971, in connection with Criminal Case No. 485-71.

THE THRILL IS GONE

Tony had told me time after time, "You need to get back into working on your case and get yourself out of here. When you do get out, you should start a business. You'd do well at that. You shouldn't be here. You're different. Most of the guys here are losers, and a lot of them will be coming back once they're released. Don't mess with drugs. Stay away from that."

The thought of starting my own business had never crossed my mind—until Tony suggested it. I had been having a good time in prison, but what I was doing was nothing of any real significance. It had kept me busy and had taken my mind off the pain I felt when I thought about my case, but that's about all.

After a good deal of reflection I felt something positive come over me. I began to sense a change in myself. It was like a burst of insight that allowed me to see things differently. I knew that if I continued the way I was going I would never get out of this place. I wanted my freedom, and I knew I had to make some changes in my life.

The incident with Ramos made me realize that continuing with the activities I was engaging in could lead to outcomes I didn't want. I wanted to get out of there and be with my son. I felt I had had enough exposure to prison life and enough experience in adjusting to it, and that it was time for me to focus on what I needed to do to improve my situation.

Lewisburg had plenty to offer, and I can't say I hadn't taken advantage of it, because I had, but I wasn't putting as much effort into working on my case as I could have or should have. I always did what I considered the best thing for myself at the time, and I don't regret that at all. I was dealing with the shame of knowing they had done this to me and the embarrassment of having been locked up for rape. The thought of it frustrated me, making me feel as if I was the victim. You would have to put yourself in my shoes to understand my feelings.

Even after I was released from the hole, the administration considered me to be a threat. They put a note in my file: "Dangerous. Keep in cellblock." I was no longer allowed in the dormitories or on the north side of the penitentiary. My movements were restricted.

In a way, I didn't care. They had already taken my freedom anyway, just by virtue of being incarcerated, and it didn't bother me to stay in the cellblocks. If I wanted to go to the other side, I would just sneak over. If I got caught they would lock me up again, but they knew I didn't consider that to be a big deal.

As soon as I had unpacked my things in the cell I went downstairs, and there was Mark. He looked at me with a smile on his face and said, "Hey partner, how you doing? It looks as if you got plenty of rest."

"I did. Now I have to check up on my shit. Come on. Let's go to the kitchen and talk."

As we were walking down the hall, I got friendly greetings from the guys walking by: "Hey Shoes, what's up? Glad you're back. Now we can get some good stuff now."

While Mark and I were sitting in the kitchen, Wayne came over and said, "Hey Shoes, I heard you were out. I have your money here." He handed me $600. "I owe you $100. I used it to try my hand in a poker game and the rest for commissary. I'll give it back to you."

"Man, don't worry about it. You don't owe me a thing," I said as I handed him a hundred-dollar bill. "Thanks. Now let me finish talking to Mark."

"Thanks, man," he said, and then walked away.

I turned my attention to Mark.

"Mark, I'm giving it up. I'm getting back into working on my case."

"I understand, man, but I'm in debt."

"That's nothing new, but I need to get back on my case."

"What the fuck did they do to you?"

I laughed.

"I'm okay. I just had a lot of time to think, and I don't want to get caught up in this."

"You're right. It's easy to get caught up in it. Shoes, you have a lot of self-discipline. I wish I had that."

"Mark, you have a lot of good qualities yourself. But that fight gave me something to think about. I could easily have found myself here for the rest of my life, and that's an outcome I definitely don't want. Besides, I'm tired of it now. The thrill is gone.

"I'll just gradually drift away from this. In the meantime, here's $500. You can have it. I have some more stashed. You can have all the stores and all the cigarettes on the north side. I have 6 stores and more than 150 cartons over there. I have it all written down. That'll be more than enough to get you out of debt. Plus you can have the football pool. They owe me money too."

"Thanks man. I understand where your head is, but you're giving up a lot. Damn! I didn't know you had *that* much."

"Well, I do, the Italians were buying all of my cigarettes. Now that they're gone I haven't been able to get rid of them as fast as I had. That's why it's so many. That's your problem now.

"I've been making a killing on the football pool, so it might be best to let Snake and Roger keep running that. As long as you're getting 10 to 15 cartons of cigarettes a week you'll have nothing to worry about."

"I didn't realize that you owned that football pool."

"Yeah, but don't tell anybody."

"Damn! Were you getting that many cartons from them?"

"I could have gotten more than that if I'd been more involved, but I stayed out of it. As long as I was able to get 10 to 15 cartons a week, it was okay with me. Listen, it would be best to have those guys on your side, so let them run it and get what you can. But if they get in a bind you got to bail them out."

"Are you going to let them know?"

"Of course, I'm going to fill you in on everything. We'll go to each of them, and I'll tell them. I've already figured it out. You can have all this shit.

"Most of all, I want to thank you for being a friend. I mean it. The guys you think you might have a problem with let me know and I'll fix it right away, because once I'm out, I'm out.

"One more thing: If you don't mind me saying so, the reason why you're always losing is that you're a poor gambler. You don't play to win. You play just because you can, and that's not good. Bet with your mind, not with your heart."

I received another reply from the court.

Sorry, we have no records of the case number you referred to in your letter.

I thought to myself, they destroyed the records, so it's just as if I had never been there.

In late January of 1974, Mark was transferred to Leavenworth, Kansas, for reasons that I never found out. I didn't get a chance to see him before he left. The administration moved him late at night.

Jim was still there. He had gotten into school and was taking some college courses. He thought of himself as a professor now and was heavily involved in chess.

I had another friend at Lewisburg, a guy by the name of Wayne. He was tall and slim, and he and I frequently worked out together, but he didn't do any running. And Jim didn't work out at all. He just stood around and talked.

Wayne was married. He wanted to introduce me to one of his wife's girlfriends, but I wasn't interested.

"She's a freak, man."

"I don't have time for that. Besides, there's nothing I could do for her as long as I'm in here."

She sent me pictures of herself. She was a nice-looking woman. She even wrote me a few letters, but what she discussed didn't interest me, things such as "Did you know you can buy pussy in the frozen food department now?" I never wrote back.

"Tell her I don't do any writing, man."

Jim said, "Man, you're crazy."

"Then you meet her. I have too many other things to do, and I'm not about to let myself get caught up in that. She's doing this only because Wayne's wife is coming up here to see him. When he leaves she'll be gone."

"How do you know she'll be gone?"

"She has only one thing on her mind: sex. Wayne said she's a freak, and I don't need that. She and I have nothing in common."

"Man, getting involved with her could make your time go by faster."

"Do you actually think I want to waste my time with that? You've got to be crazy. How long do you think that would last? I'm in here, and she's out there, where she can get all the sex she wants."

"I wish I had her."

"You can have her."

THE VISIT

One day in the fall of 1974, two guys came up to me and said, "Shoes, you have a visitor. I heard your name over the loudspeaker."

"I didn't hear anything."

"You couldn't have heard it, because you're down here in the back of the dorm, talking to Wayne. There's no speaker back here."

"Are you sure it was for me? I don't get visits. I'm not looking for nobody to comes here to see me."

"Man, we're serious. You have a visit."

"Okay."

I ignored them. Then another guy came to the back and said, "Shoes, they're up there looking for you. You have a visitor."

"Okay, thanks."

I went upstairs, but I didn't bother to wash up, brush my hair, or change my clothes, because visiting hours were almost over.

"Where have you been? We've been looking for you for a good while," said the hack.

"I didn't hear it."

"Where were you?"

"Outside, I wasn't expecting anybody."

I didn't want him to know where I had been.

As I made my way to the visiting room I wondered who it could be. I wasn't expecting anyone. When I walked into the visiting room I realized it was big, unlike the one in the Baltimore City Jail. Inmates were sitting there talking, and touching their family, friends, and loved ones. Taking pictures together and eating together.

I stood there looking around, hoping to see who had come to see me. A guy stood up on the other side of the room and waved his hand to get my attention. To my surprise, it was my cousin Dan. The last time I had seen him was about eight years earlier, when he got out of the service. He was about three years older than I. We had grown up together.

"Hi Kenzell, how you doing? I haven't seen you in years."

"Hey Dan, I'm okay. How about you?"

"I'm doing all right. Sean told me you were up here."

"How did you get in here to see me? I don't have anybody on my visiting list."

"We managed."

He smiled.

"We?"

"Oh Kenzell, this is my wife, Pat."

"Hi Pat. I'm sorry. I saw you sitting there, but I didn't know who you were. It's nice to meet you."

"Hi, I'm glad to meet you. I was just letting the two of you talk, since y'all haven't seen each other in a while and Dan has been anxious to see you."

I was taken by surprise! Pat was Caucasian, a nice-looking woman.

"I'm glad to see him too."

"It's nice to meet you. I've heard a lot about you."

"Well, don't believe everything you hear. Nobody knows that much about me."

"In any case, I'm glad to meet you."

"I'm glad to meet you too. How long have you guys been married?"

"On the tenth of May it will be three years. Isn't that right, honey?"

"Yes, that's right."

"Well, you look happy. Do y'all have children?"

"I am happy, and we have one child, a baby boy."

"Okay."

"Kenzell, I turned my life over to God, and so did Pat. We've been going to church for two years now, and I've been following Jesse Jackson. What happened to you?"

"Dan, it's good that you've turned your life over to God, but I'm not into that, and if I were I would take it very serious, but until than I'll leave it alone, and I'm not looking to follow behind anybody."

He started to get loud.

"Kenzell, what happened to you?"

"I was leaving the house on my way to work one day when two officers approached me about a robbery. They locked me up, framed me, railroaded me, charged me with rape and kidnapping, and I was given double life plus 15 years, and I was sent here to be forgotten. I never saw the woman before in my life and I don't know anything about the crime, other then what was said. Now you know what happened to me."

They were speechless for a couple seconds with their mouths open.

Kenzell, you know you can make a confession to the Judge."

"Dan, I was offered five years in return for a guilty plea, and I refused it. I am not making a confession for something I didn't do and know nothing about. Have you been listening to what I'm saying? I don't know anything about this shit."

"Kenzell, I know how you feel."

"You can't possibly know how I feel. I'm hurting inside. Every time I think about it, it hurts. I've gotten this far only by trying not to think about it, so I can build enough strength inside me to deal with it. No matter how hard I try, there isn't a day that goes by that I don't think about it. They took away my freedom. They took me away from my family and charged me with rape and kidnapping of somebody I had never seen. I lost everything I had. And I have to live with this for the rest of my life. It hurts me so bad. At first I thought I was dreaming. I didn't think it could be happening to me. You may think you know how I feel, but you have no idea."

By now I was pissed off.

"Furthermore, I do believe in God, and I have always known who God is, but I'm not interested in religion right now. What you believe in is fine as long as you're happy with it, but don't try to push it on me."

He just looked at me, speechless.

I turned to Pat and said, "As I said before it was nice meeting you."

When I got up to leave I turned to Dan and said, "Who put you up to coming here? You've got to be crazy." And I walked away.

About a week later I got a letter from Dan, saying that he and Pat would be up to see me in a week or two. He gave me his phone number and wanted me to call him.

The first chance I got, I called him. Dan answered the phone.

"Hello."

"Hi Dan, I got your letter. How you, Pat and the baby doing?"

"We're doing fine. I'm glad you called. I was wondering if you had received my letter."

"Well, now you know.

"Dan, I don't mind you coming to see me, but I don't want to talk about religion or my case, because that's something we don't see eye to eye on. As I told you before I believe in God, and I have far more faith than you can imagine. I could show you better than I could tell you over the phone. Just watch me."

"I understand, Kenzell."

"I'm serious, Dan."

"Okay."

"Can I speak to Pat?"

"Yeah, Pat telephone."

"Hello."

"Hi Pat, how you doing?"

"Hi Kenzell, I'm fine and yourself?"

"I'm okay, it was nice of you and Dan to come here and see me. I talked to Dan and told him I didn't appreciate his talking about God this and God that and asking me to make a confession. I believe in God, but I don't want anybody pushing their beliefs on me. I have enough on my mind as it is.

"This prison thing is still fairly new to me, and I think I'm dealing with it as best I can for right now. If y'all visit, I want to enjoy the moment. I'm not looking for anybody to hold my hand. I hope you understand what I'm trying to say."

"I understand, and I'll say something to Dan."

"Thank you. I have to go. My time is up. Take care."

A couple weeks later Dan and Pat came to visit again. Dan picked up right where he had left off, "It's good you believe in God. That's why you should make a confession, God will forgive you."

I ignored him and started talking to Pat.

"Pat, the reason I called last week was to ask Dan not to come up here preaching and ask me to make a confession. He gave me his word that he wouldn't do that. As you can see, his word means nothing. I can't help but wonder if somebody has put him up to this. I know God didn't. My patience is very short when it comes to that kind of reasoning. It would be wrong of me to end our visit by just walking out of here, because that's what I'm about to do. It's a shame we got off on the wrong foot."

"I'll talk to him again."

"You don't have to do that. I'm going to put a stop to it right now. It was nice meeting you.

129

I turned to Dan and said, "Please don't come up here to see me again. If you do, I won't come out. And don't write to me either. I'm sorry that it has to be this way, but I hope you understand. You take care."

"Would you like to correspond with someone?"

"No not really."

With that I left.

LETTER FROM BOSTON

A few weeks after Dan and Pat's visit I got a letter from Boston. It was from someone by the name of Jackie Davis. I didn't know anybody by that name, and I was curious as to who it was. I wasn't expecting to hear from anybody, and I rarely got any mail. I opened the letter and began to read.

> Hi!
>
> My name is Jackie Davis. I'm a friend of your cousin Dan. I thought you might like having someone to correspond with.

I thought to myself, who the hell is this?

I didn't reply to that letter.

The next day I got another letter from her and the day after that as well. I didn't respond to those either.

All sorts of thoughts ran through my mind. Perhaps the government was watching me, trying to set me up or something. I had nothing to tell them. I'd already told them all I knew.

About two weeks later Dan and Pat again came up to see me.

"I asked you not to come up here. Is there something wrong with you?"

"I'm sorry, Kenzell. I'm truly sorry. It won't happen again."

"I'm getting letters from somebody by the name of Jackie Davis. Do you know her?"

"Jackie is a friend of ours. I thought you might like to correspond with someone."

"I told you before that I wasn't interested in writing anybody. I didn't send her a reply. I thought the government was behind it, trying to set me up again. I wasn't taking any chances."

"She's a friend of mine. You can write to her if you want."

He left it at that.

I observed Pat while Dan was talking. She didn't say a thing, and I started picking up her vibes.

I suspected that Dan had been fooling around with both of these women. That Pat had gotten pregnant, and he had no choice but to marry her, which meant that Jackie was left out in the cold, and Dan found himself in a situation he hadn't anticipated, and this talk about turned his life around was a hoax. I felt very strongly about this because that lead me to think there was something he wasn't telling me. First he said Jackie is a friend of ours, than he said she's a friend of mine, that didn't set well with Pat.

"How is your mother doing, Dan?"

"She's doing fine. I talked to her last month."

"The next time you talk to her, tell her I said hello."

I was about to directed my attention to Pat. She looked as if she was drifting away.

Dan said, "It looks as though visiting hours is about over."

"I guess your right, and if you leave now you can beat the traffic. I'll see y'all later. Be safe."

"Okay Kenzell."

As I exited the visiting room I felt confident that my suspicions about Dan were true—I could sense this from Pat's body language. I didn't expect to see them again.

A few days later I got another letter from Jackie.

I haven't heard from you. You haven't answered my letters or my questions.

I still didn't write, and the next day there was another one.

I can understand that you don't want to write to someone as ugly and out of shape as I am.

I thought I would share this with Wayne and Jim, since we were close friends.

"I've received several more letters from this woman. She's a friend of my cousin. She said her name is Jackie. I have no idea what she looks like."

"Write her back."

"Where she live?"

"I don't know, her letters was mailed from Boston. I'm not going to write her. I have nothing to say to her."

"Shoes, it's not going to hurt you to write back. Just write her and say what you feel like saying."

"Ask her if she has any friends," said Jim.

"Ask her to send you a picture."

That same day I got another letter from her and a couple days later one more.

Since it didn't cost anything to write a letter, I took out a sheet of paper and wrote just one word on it: "Hi." Then I put it in an envelope and mailed it to her.

Three days later I heard from her again.

Oh, I'm so happy you wrote me back.

I thought, is she crazy or something? The only thing I said was hi, and that made her happy?

Then I decided to write her again.

I was curious about Jackie and her relationship with Dan, though I didn't mention anything about that to her, much less question her about it. I had asked myself many times who she was and what she was getting out of this. Was she so lonely that she had no one to talk to but guys in prison? After all, I couldn't satisfy her sexually, so I thought to myself, what does she want with me and what does she do?

I felt compelled to write her back and find out.

I read her letters over and over, but I couldn't pick up anything other than that she had a lot to talk about. I didn't feel as if I was in a bad dream again, but I was curious.

When I got her picture I was shocked to see that she was white. Other than Dan's wife Pat, I'd never talked to a white girl. My world had always been black.

All kinds of thoughts started running through my head. I didn't know what to make of this.

Jackie kept writing and trying to get me to write back. She had just gotten out of school and landed a job as a teacher, teaching tenth grade.

After about six months or so she wrote the following:

I've been considering going to work for Ma Bell, because they pay more than what I'm earning as a teacher. Do you think I should take a job with them?

I wrote back.

If they would pay you more, perhaps you should take a job there, but why are you asking me? You ought to know what you want to do. Who's putting you up to this?

In her next letter she said that it had been strictly her own decision to write to me.

I got into responding to her letters fairly regularly, and I eventually started telling her about my case. It always took me a while to answer her letters, because in each letter she covered a different subject. I didn't know much about writing or the subjects she was writing about, and I didn't know where to start.

I had to get a dictionary and look up a lot of words so I could comprehend what she was telling me. Writing back was hard at first, but as time went on it got easier. As soon as I answered one letter, I'd get five or six more. I couldn't keep up. Then she started writing long letters, with a dozen pages or more. I got so frustrated that I stopped opening her letters. I just let them pile up. Beside, I was still a little uncomfortable about the whole thing.

One day Jim said, "Shoes, have you ever asked Jackie if she has any friends that I could write to?"

"No. I told you I wasn't going to get into that.

"Jim, you're more curious about her than I am. You act as if you have no way to pass the time other than to horn in on things that involve me."

"Shoes, you're crazy."

"That may be true."

I stopped telling Jim what was being said. I felt as though my letters were the only thing that gave him something to look forward to, and I knew he needed to pursue some interests of his own. He apparently had no one in his life.

Wayne got letters from his wife, but he talked very little about their relationship, instead saying more about her girlfriend, the one he wanted me to meet.

The Jaycees had announced that they would be taking pictures of the inmates, so I wrote to Jackie.

If you want some pictures of me, you'll have to send me some money, because I don't have any.

Within a few days I had a reply from her saying she was sending me $50.

That really freaked me out, because she didn't know me. I wondered if she was crazy.

I received the money, and I thank you for it, but you shouldn't start something you can't handle.

She replied by saying that she liked a challenge.

I wrote her back.

I'm not sure you understand. I don't think we should start something we can't handle, and I don't particularly want to make any changes on your behalf, either in here or out there, but especially in here. I don't want you to feel any obligation toward me, and I don't want to feel anything like that toward you. You're a woman, you're human, and you have feelings. There's nothing I can provide for you while I'm here. There's only one thing we have that we can give to each other, and that's respect. I hope you understand what I'm trying to say. I know you said you do, but I want to be sure. Otherwise, it would be better to say so now, because I'd rather not discuss this again.

She replied.

You sure do know how to get your point across when you want to. I do understand, and I can handle it.

Meanwhile I had gotten away from all the other activities I had been involved in earlier at Lewisburg. A few guys teased me about the fact that I was no longer making wine.

"Shoes, you're going crazy. You're losing your mind."

"Those times are gone. I'm on another page now."

I was doing what I truly wanted to do. I even got into school, and I started thinking about my case and my future.

One day Wayne and I were in the yard working out.

"Shoes, how is Jackie? You still communicating with her?"

"Yes, I am, and things are getting better in that regard. She has shown concern for me personally. I often wonder about her, a white girl who has come into my life and shown the concern that she has. I'm impressed. At first I was scared as hell and leery of what she had in mind, but she has succeeded in engaging my interest."

"That's good, man. You need help from someone on the outside. I hope you make the best of it. I'm glad now that you didn't fool with my wife's girlfriend. She's nothing but a freak and an airhead. Knowing you, I'm sure she would have turned you off."

"I agree with you, and I didn't want to hear that stupid shit she had to say. Anyway, back to Jackie. At first she wrote only two or three pages per letter. After I started answering her, that rose to six to eight pages per letter, and then to 25 or 30 pages. She writes at least twice a month. She keeps me busy."

"What does she talk about?"

"Everything, philosophy, astrology, psychology, you name it. In between the longer letters, she writes shorter ones, anywhere from one to six pages at a time. Sometimes it takes me a week to answer one or two of her letters. That's why I haven't been out. When I'm not in my cell, I'm in the library. The strange thing about it is that despite my initial resistance I've come to like it."

"Shoes, you must be learning a lot."

"I've acquired so much knowledge that my head is about to burst. Jackie has really opened up my eyes to another world."

"I hope you succeed in getting out of here soon."

"Man, I'm determined to get out of here, with all my faculties. You can take that to the bank. I waited to hear back from the court now."

Jackie and I kept the correspondence going. I realized how ignorant I was about so many things. That's what made it interesting. Trying to keep up with her was a challenge. She was a good writer, and she was very knowledgeable. I felt as if I was draining her, because she was very smart and ran circles around me, but she never belittled me in any way. She got me into reading and writing more and researching various things. I started spending more time in the library than I had before. I eventually dropped out of school, because I wasn't learning anything there.

With Jackie's help I learned a lot. She introduced me to a whole new world of knowledge, something for which I will always be grateful. We never argued about anything, though we did have our share of debates on various topics. Other than that I just went along with her program. And when it came to my case she was very supportive of me.

The relationship went so smoothly that I thought something was wrong. I had never experienced anything like it before.

One day I was sitting in my cell, thinking about my case, when I thought of the Judge who had sentenced me. I decided to write him a letter.

Dear Mr. Leibenlot,

> I'm not writing to you to discuss my case but to tell you about myself. First of all, how are you doing? As for myself, I'm okay. You know, I used to think I was hip, but I really

didn't know anything about the law or its ramifications. I was defenseless and helpless. In fact, I was damned near illiterate. Well, things have changed. Now I feel as though I'm in college but not seeking a degree. My mind is far from that, but I'm proud of myself because I've come a long way since my trial. And I think I'm utilizing my time wisely these days. Of course I had to make choices along the way, and though I'm not perfect I think I usually chose what was best for me under the circumstances at the time.

I mailed the letter but didn't receive a response.

The following month I wrote again.

Dear Mr. Leibenlot,

How are you doing? It's me again. I've just come in after running five miles. Yes, I said running. I don't jog. I run. There is a difference, you know. Jogging requires more patience and takes a greater toll on your joints — so much so that you may be better off walking.

Anyway, after taking a shower I decided to drop you a line or two. There's something I want to share with you today. It's not that important, but I think it does have some significance.

When the hack opened the doors for breakfast this morning I was on my way outside, to go running. As I passed him he said, "Evans, go back and close your door." I replied, "That isn't my job." And I continued walking.

When I came back inside and headed toward my cell he said, "You haven't changed at all. You're just as arrogant as ever."

Without saying a word I went back upstairs to my cell. I

could tell he was furious, but I didn't care, because I'm not here to do his job.

On my way to the shower I thought about what he had said and smiled. He must have noticed the change in me. And I hope he realized that it was his job to walk down the hallway to check and close all the doors behind everybody.

I still got no response from the judge.

I continued writing to him, roughly once a month. From his lack of response, I figured he felt that he was above writing to me, but eventually he wrote back.

It's good that you're doing okay. If you don't mind, I'm going to have your letters put in your file.

I was excited, not so much about the nature of his reply but simply because of the fact that he had responded at all.

Because I spent a great deal of time in the library, some of the other inmates would come to me and ask, "Would you help me write a letter to the Judge?"

"Help you how? I can get you a book that shows you how to write a letter, but you have to say what *you* want in it."

"Shoes, I can't read. I'll pay you."

"I don't want your money. Why don't you get yourself into school and learn to read and write?"

It was hard to imagine that there were guys who were married and had families and had never even learned how to read and write.

"I feel embarrassed and ashamed of myself."

"You're not the only one here with that problem. There are a lot of others here who can't read or don't know how to write a letter. In fact, everybody in here has *some* kind of problem. And just like you, they're ignoring it too."

When I got to know these guys better I wrote letters for them. They cried about every little thing. It made me think about what Mark had said: *They can do the crime, but they don't want to do the time.*

They were guilty as hell too. The older inmates were worse than the younger ones.

MEETING JACKIE

I wanted to meet Jackie in person, and asked her about a letter I wrote to her in October of 1974.

"Would you come to Lewisburg to see me?"

"Sure I will, but not until we get to know each other better."

"Okay. It's a deal."

We continued writing, and she started her new job with Ma Bell and liked it there. She also came to see me. And when she did, she stayed two days because of the long drive from Boston to Lewisburg. I often asked myself, what the hell is going on? Why is she in my life?

I was trying to keep the relationship in perspective — and honest. I didn't know what she expected to get out of it.

One day I asked, "What do you expect from this relationship?"

"I just want an open, honest, sincere, and frank relationship. I am getting something out of it, and I hope you are too."

I felt as if there was something unusual about my relationship with Jackie, because everything was going so smoothly, perhaps too smoothly. I kept telling myself I had to be careful, because it didn't seem real. It was almost too good to be true.

I still couldn't figure out why she was interested in me. For quite some time it was hard for me to comprehend what was going on, because I thought she was being much too good to me. I felt I didn't deserve someone like her, and I never really got over my suspicion that there was something or someone behind it all.

One day I was in the cafeteria, eating dinner and thinking about various things, when Jim came over to my table.

"Hey Shoes, what's up?"

"Nothing, I was just thinking."

"Thinking about what?"

"Life is so beautiful when people take the time to understand one another. When we let down our guard, dismantle our defenses, and remove the walls that divide us, we can release all the stress and sit back and appreciate the fact that the burden we've been carrying around for so long has been lifted from our shoulders."

"Man, what are you talking about?"

"I'm just thinking out loud."

The next time Jackie came to visit me I started discussing my case with her.

"The court just denied my motion on a technicality."

"Why don't you pursue a different avenue?"

"Well, I've been working on another issue regarding incompetent attorney because my court-appointed attorney was incompetent. I've discovered a lot of evidence that he withheld. They say that issue may be difficult to prove, but there are cases where it's been done. I've researched a lot of cases that were reversed on issues similar to in my case, some almost identical to it. I want to take my time with this, to make sure I cover everything. I've learned from my mistakes."

"How about if I go and see F. Lee Bailey? He's based in Boston."

"I'm not really interested in him, because he's a trial lawyer, I don't think he could help me. Besides, I don't have much confidence in lawyers right now."

When I left the visiting room I talked to some guys who had used him, and they felt he was good at certain things.

When I came out for my visit with Jackie the next day, we picked up where we had left off.

Jackie said, "I'd like to go see Bailey after all. What do we have to lose?"

I figured this was one way of testing her, to see if she was sincere.

"Okay, if that's what you want me to do."

After she got back home she went to see him, and then she wrote, "He wants a $5,000 retainer."

"I don't have any money."

"I'll put it up for you."

"I really appreciate that."

Her willingness to put up the money made me realize that she was indeed serious. That really blew my mind!

I constantly thought about her offer, right up until the time she was due to make contact with him again. Then I called her.

"Hi Jackie, how you doing?"

"Hi! It's so good to hear your voice!"

I smiled.

"You would hear it every day if I had any say in the matter."

"That would be great."

"I have only a few minutes. I'm calling to tell you not to go and see Bailey after all. I've been thinking hard about that. Don't do it. He's not what I need. He's a trial lawyer. Guys in here who used him say he won a lot of cases by having them cop a plea or make some sort of deal. They claim that all he wants is money. He would be a waste of our time and your money. Let's forget about him."

"If that's what you want, I'll stop pursuing it."

"Thanks. I'll write you tonight. I love you."

"I love you too."

I was never this close with my wife. My relationship with Jackie was entirely different. Every month she would make the long trip down here from Boston, not wanting to disappoint me, and she was always on time.

Whenever I asked her to send me money, it came promptly — so promptly that I could bank on it. I knew if she said she was going to do something, she would do it. I was really grateful to her for that, and I loved her for it. I felt very special to have someone like her. Being confined and having someone like her on the outside, someone who would do all the things I asked, was a blessing. I felt I was being selfish at times, but she never complained. She was a true friend.

"Do you know what next Monday is?" I asked her the next time we spoke.

"Next Monday? Let me think. It's not a holiday."

"It's our anniversary. We've been together for two years. I'm taking off next week. I'll see you Monday morning at nine."

"Okay, I'll see you on Monday."

When Jackie came down to see me, the first thing she said was, "Congratulations! We've made it through another year."

"Congratulations! We sure have. Thank you."

We kissed.

"You're welcome. I love you."

"I love you too."

"I've been talking to a palm reader."

"What?"

"Don't you believe in palm readers?"

"I don't know. I think some people have greater insight than others. What did she say?"

"She said I was involved with a man who wore a uniform. She doesn't deal with colors and couldn't tell what color the uniform was. She went on to say that I wouldn't be able to get with you right away, but that you would be with me near the end of 1976. But to be sure of the reading, she said she would need more information about you as well as something personal that belongs to you."

"Do you believe all of that?"

"I don't know. I didn't tell her a thing about myself, and a lot of things she said were true."

"I haven't gotten anywhere on my case. In fact, I haven't heard anything more about it. I don't want to get my hopes up too high. It sure would be nice to hear something good, but the way things have been going, we don't know what might happen."

It was on a cold morning in February of 1976, that Jackie came up to visit me again.

"Tell me about that palm reader. Have you talked to her again?"

"No, I haven't."

"I was in the law library researching more cases on incompetent attorneys, and I came cross a case regarding the Youth Act. I read more about it and realized it applied to me. After researching it further, I prepared a motion and I filed it with the District Court. I can't help but wonder if that motion will bring about my release from prison."

As time went on I kept in mind what Jackie was told by that palm reader. She said to me, "You've got to have faith."

"I do have faith, and I'm very optimistic about this. I believe anything is possible."

EDUCATING MYSELF

I joined the NAACP and the Jaycees. This was the first time I had ever taken part in any organization. I recalled Jackie telling me that she liked a challenge, so I took on the challenge at hand.

I got into arts and crafts, but I thought it was too boring and I didn't seem to be getting anything out of it. I enrolled in two computer courses, but they didn't interest me. I liked psychology and philosophy.

I had always liked running. I was running five miles a day and working out every day, even in rain or snow.

The track wasn't very good, but I was still fast. I ran the dashes, the quarter-mile, and the mile, and I did distance running as well. I clocked a mile at 3 minutes 52 seconds. I had no serious competitors at the time, though I did compete against students from Penn State, Bucknell, and a few other schools in the area.

I wrote a letter to the Olympic Commissioner and asked for permission to try out for the 1976 Olympics, but they informed me that they don't allow criminals to participate. That was very discouraging. I felt I was running at my peak at that time, and I wanted to show the world how fast I was.

I was awarded a lot of trophies at Lewisburg, which made me feel good, but after being turned down for the Olympics I gave most of them away. I did send some of the trophies to my son, and I kept running, just for the exercise.

I went through a lot of books and spent a lot of time studying.

As I returned to my cell one day after my run, I noticed a box and a letter on my bed. The letter was from Jackie, but there was no indication of who had sent the box. On opening it, what I beheld was a set of twelve "Personal Power" books. I read Jackie's letter and responded. Among other things, I thanked her for the books.

I started looking through them. Each one covered a different topic — topics such as personal power, thought power, creative power and spiritual power to name a few. I got right into them. I had to read each book about three times to acquire a good understanding of what it was saying. They were very profound. I had never read any books like them before, and I could see and feel myself changing from the knowledge they conveyed.

I knew that if I conquered all the knowledge in these books, I just might be capable of walking through walls. That's how powerful I thought they were. I definitely knew I wasn't the same person that I had been when I arrived here at Lewisburg, but I had kept quiet about it. I was finding it harder to communicate with and relate to some of the other inmates. We were no longer on the same wavelength. They often didn't understand what I was talking about, and I didn't care. They thought I was losing my mind and going crazy, but I was actually having a good time and learning an awful lot.

I thought quite a bit about the future, and of what I was going to do when I got out. I was always hearing stories from guys who had returned, saying that there are no jobs out there or that it's really hard to find one. Those stories always stuck in my mind, because I wanted to be prepared for the day when I would be released. I knew I needed money to survive, and I figured that if I came up with a good enough idea it would solve that problem. I would never have thought of that if it hadn't been for reading the books I had received.

One day when I was in the yard working out I started doing a certain exercise with a bar that I always used, and I thought I might be able to develop it into an exercise device. It was a simple exercise that deals with your inner strength, and it was effective. Guys were always coming around watching, and one of them asked, "What kind of exercise can I do? I just want to tone up without using weights."

"I do calisthenics, by using just my natural strength. If you used this bar the right way, you could get results rather quickly. The more you use it, the sooner you will see results. All you need to do is use it for 15 minutes every day over a period of two weeks."

"You look as if you're in good shape. Did you get like that just from using the bar?"

"No. I also run, and I do push-ups, sit-ups, and pull-ups. The bar tones and shapes the body and stretches it. I can show you how to get the best results from it."

A few guys took to using the bar, and I started working with them, monitoring the time they put in and taking notes. As I did this I was developing my model, but I didn't mention that to them. It took me about seven or eight months to finish it, including diagrams illustrating how to use the device effectively.

I wrote a letter to the U.S. Patent Commissioner requesting a handbook on the procedure for filing a patent application. They sent me one. I went to the library, got a D.C. phone book, and looked up the names and addresses of ten patent attorneys in Washington. I composed a letter explaining my situation and requesting assistance in obtaining patent protection. I sent the letter to each of them.

I was also working on another invention, one that was entirely different from the first one and a lot more complicated. This was for something everybody could use. I made two models of it, but the hacks shook down my cell and destroyed them. I went into the plumbing shop to learn about pressure and how it works, and I read up on various materials that I might be able to use. I eventually realized that I had put far too much time into this, and I began to feel that I wasn't in the right environment to bring it to fruition. I knew I needed some help, so I wrote to Sears Roebuck and American Standard. They both told me they had been working on something similar to what I had described, and they wanted me to send them what I had. I wasn't about to do that, because I had no protection.

When Jackie came down to see me I kept her abreast of everything that was going on.

"By the way, I didn't send you any books."

"Well if you didn't send them, I have no idea who did, but I'm keeping them. They're my Bible."

I began to feel as though the penitentiary was shrinking or that I was outgrowing it. I was tired of seeing the very same guys two, three, or four times a day — sometimes more — and listening to them saying the same things over and over: "Hey man, how you doing?" and "What's up?" That was essentially the extent of their conversation. It was as if they were robots. I wondered how anybody could remain in that state of mind, day in and day out, for years.

I took to avoiding them, by turning and heading in a different direction whenever I saw them coming, but I realized that that was a waste of my time and energy. From that time on I just walked right past them, saying nothing, and went on about my business.

That led them to think that I was losing it.

One evening I ran into Wayne in the yard.

"Hey Shoes, what's going on? They're saying you're losing it."

"I'm not obligated to say anything to them. The next time, ask them what they think my problem is or what I should do about it. I bet they won't be able to tell you. They might even say something stupid.

"I really don't have much in common with them as far as 'time' goes either. Some of them are serving only five, ten, or fifteen years here, twenty at the most. I'm facing life. Some of them have been released and are back, talking that same old stuff. Man, I'm not about to let them do their time off me."

"You're right about that," said Wayne. "When they get out of here, they won't be thinking about you."

"And neither will you."

"I suppose you're right about that."

"Of course, you and I come from the same neighborhood, so I guess that makes it a little different for us, but if you get out and then come back here I won't have anything to do with you. Look at Jim. He's been gone for over three months now. Before he left he was talking about sending pictures. I haven't heard from him. Have you? Not that I care about getting pictures from him. After all, I didn't ask him for any. But if he ever ends up back here, I'm not messing with him. That applies to you too."

"I know that, but I'm not coming back. Not if I can help it."

Two weeks later Wayne went home. He said, "I'll keep in touch, man."

"You don't need to keep in touch with me. You take care of yourself, and make sure you don't come back. I'll see you when I get out."

"Okay Shoes."

One Sunday morning I was going out for my run when I walked past the chapel and stumbled into one of Jim's born-again Christian brothers.

"Good morning, Brother Shoes. Would you like to join us for Sunday service?"

"No thanks, I *am* going to service right now."

"Brother Shoes, it looks to me as if you're going jogging."

"I'm going out to run and exercise."

"Today is Sunday. You should give this day to God."

"I give every day to God."

I went on down the hall and out the door to the yard. As I was walking I thought about the period when I was into hustling, and about the Muslim guy named Jay who would pull me to the side and ask me to slip him a pork chop. I just walked on, smiling.

One day I got to thinking about religion, and decided that I would participate, but just to understand what it was all about, for my own personal gain. I didn't let them know my motives.

I didn't plan to become an adherent of any particular faith. I studied with the Sunni (Orthodox) Muslims and the Black Muslims, as well as with the Catholics and the evangelical Christians. I started going to church, participating in the services, fasting, praying, and doing everything they were doing.

I didn't spend a lot of time with any of those groups. All of them wanted me to join, and some were more persistent than others, but I refused. I had a program that I stuck with every day.

SENTENCE REDUCTION

In September of 1976, I received a letter from the court. I was hoping it would be something favorable. I opened it and read the last line: "Your motion has been denied." I had a lot of confidence riding on that motion, and I knew I was right, but the judge denied it as he done with the ones in the past but this time I'm going to appeal it. The next day, I couldn't wait to get to the library. I prepared another motion and filed it with the Court of Appeals. I was optimistic, thinking I might be released, based on what that palm reader had told Jackie. And that was the only thing I had in court. I should have appealed that last one.

I wrote to Jackie.

The Judge denied my motion, but he gave no reason for the denial, I'm appealing his decision. I still think about what the palm reader told you, and I have my hopes up about being released from prison. I feel very strongly about that issue.

After about five or six weeks I received a reply from the Court of Appeals saying that my case had been remanded to the District Court.

You are entitled to protection under the Youth Act, and the District Court Judge will have to reconsider your case.

This was described as an "unpublished decision."

I called Jackie right away. While the phone was ringing I thought to myself, damn. Why didn't I appeal those motions he denied. He was just being an ass.

"Hello."

"Hi baby, I have some good news! The Court of Appeals remanded my case to the District Court, saying that I was entitled to protection under the Youth Act and that the District Court has to reconsider my case. The order was described as an 'unpublished decision.' I don't understand why it was classified that way. I guess they don't want the lower courts flooded with cases involving the Youth Act."

Jackie was excited too.

"I'm coming down to see you, and we can talk about getting an attorney to handle the case in the District Court."

"I'm not too happy about getting an attorney. I've done all the work that's needed, and I'm afraid an attorney might screw it up. Besides, I can't put much faith in a lawyer, based on the experience I had with my court-appointed lawyer. At that time I was quite ignorant of legal matters, and I knew that the government was paying him."

"I'm willing to pay for an attorney."

"Let's wait and see what happens."

"Okay. I'm still coming down next week."

"Good. I'll see you then. I love you."

"I love you too. And by the way, is there anything you need?"

"No, I'm okay."

"All right, I'll see you."

Months had gone by and there was no response from the District Court, I got anxious and filed a petition for a writ of mandamus, and filed in the court of appeals too, compelling to act on the motion.

In the meantime I had been spending a lot of time in the library and one day I got to talking with another inmate—a guy from Baltimore—about the issue. He said, "I know of a lawyer who knows that Judge, and he's pretty good."

"He doesn't need to do any work, because I've already done it all myself. But since he knows the Judge, maybe he can get them to speed things up."

"It helps to have someone there to persuade him. You might have pissed him off by filing that petition for a writ of mandamus."

"I tend to doubt that. I'm guessing that he denied it without even looking at it."

"You seem to know a lot about the issue."

"I do. Let me have his name and address."

"His name is Freddy Wilson. I'll bring you his address and phone number tomorrow."

"Thanks."

I wrote Jackie and gave her all the information. She called the attorney and arranged everything. He even came up to Lewisburg to visit me.

"Hi. I'm Freddy Wilson. How are things going?"

"Hi. I'm Kenzell Evans. Pleased to meet you. I'm doing okay. Are you familiar with the Youth Act?"

"Yes, I am."

"Here's a copy of everything pertaining to my case in regard to the Youth Act."

"What are you expecting?"

"I expect to be released right away or at least relatively soon, considering that I've already served six years. Under the Youth Act, my sentence should have been eight to twelve years."

"Based on the conversation I had with Ms. Davis, I gather you would like me to speak to the Judge on your behalf. I did receive all your material and I went through that and did some additional research of my own. You have a strong case, and you're right on target. You are definitely giving the Judge something to think about. I know him, and he can be stubborn. As you may know, he's the chief Judge."

"Why do you think it was classified as an 'unpublished decision'?"

"Well, *you* found it, didn't you? Then *others* could find it too. Classifying it as unpublished may have been the court's way of avoiding any obligation to inform you — and countless others — of the possibility that the Youth Act could be brought to bear in your case."

"In other words, it would flood the courts if they informed everyone to whom the Youth Act applies."

"That's right. Mr. Evans, I can't promise you anything, but I'll do the best I can for you and I'll keep you informed."

"Okay. I can't ask for any more than that."

About a month later in August, 1977, I got a letter from the lawyer.

I met with the Judge on two occasions to speak on your behalf concerning the Youth Act. Your sentence has been reduced to 35 years. I know you were expecting a lesser sentence. Fortunately, you're in a better situation than you were before, and you will be seeing the parole board soon. Good luck.

I called Jackie to break the news to her.

"Hello."

"I heard from the lawyer yesterday."

She was excited.

"What did he say?"

"My sentence was reduced to 35 years, and I'll be seeing the parole board soon."

"That's good. It's certainly a lot better than what you had before. How soon will you be seeing the parole board?"

"I don't know. I guess they'll be getting in contact with me."

"You don't sound too confident. What's wrong?"

"I was hoping to be released. I guess I got overanxious, thinking about what the palm reader told you. Maybe I screwed it up by getting the lawyer involved. What I'm really thinking about is you, us."

"What do you mean by that?"

"We'll have to discuss that later. I have to go now. I love you."

"I love you too."

In the meantime I sent Willie copies of the motions I had filed so he could follow suit. He hadn't done a single thing all along. I had done all the research and the filings, and I made sure that he got copies of everything. I had even typed up the transcript and the briefs and given him a copy, so he could reap the same rewards I did if there were any.

TRANSFER TO ATLANTA

It was in the spring of 1977 that I started picking up strange vibes in my relationship with Jackie. The pace wasn't quite the same as before.

She had said to me a while back, "I met a guy by the name of Harry, from England. I told him all about you, and he insists on talking to me."

"You know that this puts me at a disadvantage."

"There's no need to worry about him. He's just somebody to talk to."

"Since he's from another country, I figure he's seeking to gain something or other, he has an ulterior motive."

I also didn't think Jackie was strong enough to handle this, so I backed off. I felt I was losing her, but I couldn't tell her that, because I didn't want her to think of me as being selfish. She was human and had feelings of her own. She was entitled to live her life as she pleased.

I remembered what I had said to her early in the relationship: *I don't think we should start something we can't handle.* I thought this was one of the biggest hurdles to overcome in a relationship in which one party or the other is confined.

Besides, this guy Harry had the upper hand. He was able to be with her every day, and may have read my letters when she wasn't around.

I asked her about that very thing. A few days later she wrote me.

On several occasions I caught him reading your letters, and I asked him not to do that anymore.

I started referring to Harry as the Joker. Jackie and I continued our correspondence, but as time went on I could feel our relationship losing its strength. I felt she was enjoying two worlds, and I didn't want to get caught up in that. Of course I was hurt, but I didn't want to go down that road.

We had talked about so many things, including having a future together once I was released. Now I was trying to get her out of my mind, because I didn't want to worry over her or deal with the fact that someone else had taken my woman.

To my surprise, I received a letter from William, my cousin from North Carolina. Dan's older brother, he was 4 years older then me. I was happy to hear from him. He wrote to say,

I saw your daddy the other day. He's still the same. When you have a chance, give me a call. Enclosed is my number.

I couldn't believe what I had read. That was the first time I had ever had any mention of "my daddy." I knew he wasn't talking about Bruce Evans.

That stayed on my mind for a good while. It was something new for me to think about. I was very curious, so I wrote him back.

What do you mean by "my daddy?" Where did you get that from?

He replied, you can see him when you get out. In the meantime, call me.

As time went on, the institution continued to change. It had grown to about 1,550 inmates, a number that was expected to increase even further. Now the population was about 90 percent black, and growing. Inmates were being transferred into the federal system from the Lorton Correctional Institution Complex, a facility owned and operated by the District of Columbia but located in Virginia.

There were more assaults and killings occurring here now than ever before. They started putting up bars everywhere, which made it look like a zoo. The library was downsized with no more free stamps and stationery. And the quality of the food, which was quite good when I arrived, had been declining.

It was during the summer of 1978, I felt I needed a change, a fresh start. I went to see my caseworker, a Mr. Stonewall. He was a young white guy — or at least looked very young, almost like someone who had just gotten out of high school. He made an effort to appear tough, but he wasn't. He was green. Somebody must have told him to act that way, because he didn't seem to know much.

"Mr. Stonewall, I would like to be transferred to Atlanta. I have outgrown this place. Do you think you could arrange that for me?"

"Mr. Evans, I don't think so. You have no valid reason to be transferred."

"What kind of reason do I need?"

"You need some kind of hardship."

"What are you talking about?"

"I can't transfer you just like that. Besides, I have more important things to do."

I went to see my counselor, Mr. Light. We had known each other since I arrived at Lewisburg. Mr. Light was a lieutenant back then. Now he was my counselor, and an assistant to Mr. Stonewall.

"Mr. Light, can you help me get transferred? I went to see Mr. Stonewall, and I got nowhere with him. I would like to be transferred to Atlanta. I think I've been here long enough. I'm tired of seeing the same faces, all day every day. I need a change of scenery."

"Sure you do, and you're right. I've known you for a long time, and you've done well here. It's amazing how you have changed. I would hate to see you turn sour again. I'll do what I can to see that you're on the next bus out of here. And I'll take this opportunity to wish you well, in case I don't see you again."

"Thank you, Mr. Light."

"Sure Evans."

I didn't want Jackie worrying about me, so I wrote her,

> I'm writing to tell you that I've requested a transfer to Atlanta. I don't want you to worry about me.

She wrote back,

> Atlanta is so far away that I would have to fly there to visit you. That would be expensive, and I wouldn't be able to stay very long.

> About a week later on a Wednesday evening I was told I would be leaving on a bus to Atlanta in the morning.

Again I wrote her,

> Don't worry about traveling to visit me in Atlanta. I'll be okay. I'd always thought that nothing would ever come between us, but that was a fantasy. I love you. Take care.

I put that letter in the mail the night before I left.

It was in September of 1978, when I got on the bus leaving for Atlanta. All kinds of thoughts went through my mind.

Among other things, it was hard to keep my mind off of Jackie. It wasn't as if I was running away from Jackie. I just didn't want to get caught up in that kind of relationship. I thought it would be best to move on with my life. Besides, I would be depriving her of her life if I remained involved with her.

After being in Lewisburg for seven years, I was finally getting a chance to see what it was like on the other side of the wall. When I arrived there, I hadn't thought of paying close attention to the things that surrounded the prison.

I got to thinking about the wine and sandwiches I had made, the gambling and stealing I had engaged in, my stays in the hole, and the violence that had taken place. Those things had given me extensive exposure to the compound. I had seen the population turn over two or three times. When I came to Lewisburg 90 percent of the population was white and 10 percent was black. Now it's about the opposite.

Lots of guys wasted their time at Lewisburg, playing ball and lying to each other about who they were or the people and possessions they had left behind. Some of them claimed to have a Cadillac and some girls. When it was time to go home their minds were blank. And many of them returned, all with the same tale: *I couldn't find a job.*

I thought about Tony, Wayne, Jim, and especially Mark, my hustling partner. I hope he's doing okay. I also thought about Jimmy Hoffa, and the spy from Russia, and the mayors, lawyers, the preachers, and so many others.

When the bus arrived at the penitentiary in Atlanta, it was raining and gloomy. The warden came out, got on the bus, and looked at us.

"Please remain seated until I tell you to do otherwise."

He then proceeded to walk down the aisle of the bus, looking to the left and to the right, pointing his finger at each of us individually and saying either "You stay seated" or "You can get up."

When he got to the back of the bus, he turned around and came back up the aisle to the front. Then he said, "Those of you whom I told to stay seated, remain on the bus. And if I missed somebody, you'd better stay seated as well, for your own safety. This is the federal penitentiary in Atlanta, GA. There are hard-core criminals here: murderers, rapists, etc. Guys from Alcatraz, Leavenworth, you name it. They wouldn't think twice about killing you. The ones I told to stay seated, you don't belong here. I don't know why they sent you. The inmates here would make faggots out of you. I don't want to see that happen, so I'm going to leave you on the bus."

One of the marshals who had accompanied us said, "We have orders to bring them here."

"I don't care. They're not staying here. Take them back where they came from, because their lives aren't worth a quarter here. They'll either be killed or turned into homosexuals. There's too much going on here now. I have no control of it once they get behind these walls. I'll say it again: If I missed anybody, you'd better stay seated. The rest of you, move on out."

About six or seven guys stayed on the bus. The rest of us got off and proceeded to the main building. The hallways were so long and wide that they looked more like streets or alleys. There were cellblocks on both sides of the hallway. They too were large, and there were inmates in the halls and the cellblocks, hollering like animals at a zoo.

"That's my bitch. That's my bitch right there," I heard one say.

As I came through the doorway, a lot of guys started calling my name: "Shorty Big Shoes! Shorty Big Shoes! Do you need anything, man? We're going to get some good wine now. He's the winemaker. He knows how to make it."

A lot of them knew me from Lewisburg, so in that sense I felt welcome here. But what they didn't know is that I was no longer into winemaking.

We proceeded to Receiving and Discharge. After going through R & D we were allowed into the general population. I started looking around, feeling the place out. I was impressed by the size of it. It was huge, like a small city. You could set Lewisburg inside it and still have plenty of room left over. The population was three times that of Lewisburg.

I was assigned to "A" block. It was a large one. In fact, all of the blocks here were large and had at least six to eight inmates to a cell. They were more serious minded here than at Lewisburg, and the place was much older. They fed you well, much better than at Lewisburg. You could never say you didn't get enough to eat. They served meals all day long and half the night. There were three shifts in the kitchen. There were two and a half shifts in the textile mill each day. You could work three shifts if you could manage. You could work as many hours as you wanted, and you never had a chance to meet everybody. It wasn't unusual to meet someone and then not see them again for months, except those who were on the same schedule as you. Or you might think that someone had just arrived, only to find out that they'd already been there for quite some time, perhaps years.

On my first day I was locked up for being in the wrong block at count time. I had been talking with a friend and had forgotten about the count. I was sent to solitary confinement for three days. When I got out I was told to report to the kitchen, where they assigned me to cleaning tables after breakfast, a job that took all of 15 minutes a day.

One of the guys who had come down with me from Lewisburg was assigned to "B" block. He was soon killed by another inmate, for playing his radio too loud after the guy told him several times to turn it down.

That reminded me of what the warden had said. Perhaps that guy should have stayed on the bus. He didn't last two weeks. He was young and stupid, the kind that wanted to act tough.

BREAKING UP

I eventually received a response from one of the ten attorneys to whom I had sent the letter in regard to obtaining patent protection. It had been forwarded to me from Lewisburg, and a letter from Jackie.

The attorney introduced himself and said I would need $200 to cover the patent application fee.

Since I had no money, I ultimately decided to call Jackie.

"Hello."

"Hi Jackie, how you doing?"

"Hi Kenzell, I'm all right. How are you?"

"I'm okay. An attorney contacted me and wants $200 to cover the patent application fee. He's willing to do the rest at no cost."

"I'll send you the money to cover the application fee. I know you don't have it."

"Could you?"

"Sure, I'll send you the money, and I wish you luck with that. Did you get my letter?"

"Yes, I did. What do you expect me to say? You allowed this to happen. It was your doing, not mine. You know, when you start something, you're supposed to deal with it, not push it to the side and ignore it. Otherwise, it ends up causing problems for somebody else. You said you could handle it. Sometimes it's best to leave things as they are."

"Harry's just somebody to talk to."

"I understand."

"You're much stronger than he is."

"Sweetheart, I don't want to discuss it."

"All right, I'll do something about it."

"You have said that several times before, and that's not like you."

"You're right, but I will this time."

Well, I have to go. They're telling me to get off the phone. I'll write you tonight. I love you."

"I love you too."

I went back to my cell to write her a letter.

A few days went by with no word from Jackie. This wasn't like her. I sat in my cell practically all day, thinking of how nice it had been with her and how she had let the Joker come between us. I knew he wasn't the right person for her, but he was her choice.

I wrote Jackie again, but I got no reply. This was unusual. I thought she was gone. I waited another week and wrote again, and still didn't hear from her. I thought about calling her, but it wasn't my week to call. Then I thought to myself, if I called her and the Joker answered the phone, it would just make matters worse. It would probably be best to get over her.

After waiting a few more days and didn't hear from her I decided to get rid of some personal property that I no longer needed. I started throwing things in the trash. I never did like keeping a lot of stuff I wasn't using. I got a box and gathered up all of her letters and pictures and put them in the box. There were lots of those. Also, I had been collecting stamps. I put those in the box as well.

I mailed the box to her and then wrote her a letter.

The very next day I was called to my caseworker's office. His name was Mr. Bolden. A short, fat white man, he was younger than I.

Mr. Evans, "Who is Jackie?"

"She's a friend. Why?"

"She sent you $200, and I want to make sure it's intended for you."

"What? This letter is nearly two weeks old. Why are you just now giving it to me? Why are you reading letters and holding them?"

He didn't say anything. He just reached into his drawer and pulled out three more letters from her.

"Why is she sending you that much money? Is she white?"

"Excuse me?"

"Where did you meet her?"

"I don't think that's any of your business."

My first thought was that this guy was a racist. However, I spontaneously revamped my thoughts, took my letters, and left. I wanted to avoid a no-win altercation. There was no point in me getting upset about him reading my mail. That was just one of the games they played.

I was upset about having mailed that box to Jackie. I had done that only because I thought she was gone. There was no way I could retrieve the box now.

When I got back to my cell I read her letters. She was upset too, saying she hadn't heard from me. The caseworker had evidently held the letters I wrote to her.

I called Jackie the first chance I got.

"Hello."

"Hi."

"How could you?"

"I'm very sorry. I thought you were gone. My caseworker called me into his office two days ago and gave me your letters. He had held them for two weeks, and I had no way of knowing. He probably held mine too. Did you get my letters?"

"Yes, four letters, together with a box of pictures, old letters, and stamps."

"Well, I didn't send those letters all at the same time. If you notice, they all have different dates. By the way, I have received the money. Thanks so much for that."

"You don't realize the tremendous impact that you've had on me."

There were lots of days when I thought about her, but I eventually managed to see our relationship for what it was and I moved on. The last time we talked in Lewisburg, I felt it coming. I was just glad that I was no longer there by the time it broke off, but I had no way of knowing it would happen the way it did. Though, I knew I had made the right decision at the right time, and I had no regrets.

I got in touch with the patent attorney and sent him the money. I later got a response from him.

The patent examiner believes your patent is similar to those of several other inventors. I insisted that it wasn't, and I'm sending you illustrations of the patents that he was referring to.

I got in touch with the patent examiner and contested his assertion that my invention was like the others. We went back and forth for about two months. I worked on it diligently day and night, covering all specifications in great detail. I had no time for anything else. There were days when I neither ate nor left my cell, other than for my work in the kitchen. My mind was focused on trying to obtain a patent. After submitting what I considered to be the final version, I didn't hear from him anymore.

BACK TO LEWISBURG

At first I liked Atlanta. I met a lot of inmates, people from all over the country. They were there for all kinds of crimes. Some were gangsters from the Capone days, just biding their time and waiting to die.

Unlike Lewisburg, there was always somebody being assaulted or killed. I recalled that when incidents of that kind occurred at Lewisburg the entire penitentiary was locked down. In Atlanta they just told you to move to the side, and two guys would come in with a stretcher, pick up the body, and take it away. Someone would come in behind them with a mop and bucket, to mop up the blood, at which point everything would return to normal. Nothing ever stopped. Everything just moved right along.

After being in Atlanta for over a year, I decided to get my GED. I took a few classes too: computer programming, business, and accounting. As time went on, however, the place began to bore me. I wondered why. I started observing everything more closely and came to the conclusion that Atlanta was essentially a large graveyard that housed senior citizens.

The pace was slow, and nobody talked about time. The atmosphere was laid back, like a retirement home. I never heard anybody talk about the parole board or about getting out. I found it depressing, and I wondered if the other inmates ever looked at it that way. To hear them talk, you would think there were lots of things going on.

The sick line was amazing to see. You'd have to see it to believe it. Every day, three times a day, there were over 250 inmates in line for medication. The line started at the hospital, continued alongside two other buildings, and ended at the recreation building.

They were getting Thorazine, Valium, and no telling what else. Many of them walked around all day like zombies. You would see them standing around and talking to themselves, saying things like the following:

"I killed that bitch."

"Shut up bitch, or I'll stab you again."

"I'm going to kill him too. Just wait till I see him again."

"When I get out, I'm going to kill that MF — and his family."

"Hey man, give me a cigarette."

"Shut up bitch. Don't you see us talking?"

This went on all day every day. Maybe that's why they were transferring younger people in, to liven the place up. I wanted out of there. I went to my caseworker and said, "Mr. Bolden, I would like to be transferred."

"Where do you want to be transferred to?"

"Anywhere except Lewisburg."

"I'm sorry. There's a freeze on all transfers right now."

"Well, when the freeze is lifted would you keep me in mind?"

"I'll do that."

"Thank you."

On leaving his office I thought to myself, that lying MF!

A month later there was talk of Atlanta closing, followed by talk of moving Cubans into Atlanta. Inmates were running around talking about getting transferred out, to various institutions. I rushed over to see my caseworker and asked to be transferred back to Lewisburg. At that point I really didn't care where I went. I was ready to go. I was tired of Atlanta. At least I'd had some time to get over my breakup with Jackie.

My request was granted, January, 1981 I found myself on my way back to Lewisburg. It was a nice sunny day, not raining as it had been on the day I arrived in Atlanta. The bus was full, unlike the one in which I had been brought to Atlanta. I'd been looking forward to that earlier transfer, but now I was anxious to get away. I lay back and checked out the scenery, the new cars, and the buildings.

Back then I had felt the need for a change in my life. After being in Atlanta, however, I wouldn't recommend it to anybody who had a choice in the matter. It felt like a death hole to me. Once you were there, they threw away the key and forgot about you.

I dozed off to sleep. I was tired.

By the time I woke up, the bus had arrived at Lewisburg. After everybody had gone through orientation and was assigned to their cells, it looked as though everyone from Atlanta was in Lewisburg. Two busloads of us had been transferred here that day. Others had been transferred to various institutions all over the country, except for the older inmates. I think they may have stayed at Atlanta.

I hadn't been back a week when my old caseworker, Mr. Stonewall, called me into his office.

"You wanted to see me?"

"Yes. I see that you accomplished a few things while you were in Atlanta. That's good. May I ask what made you change your mind and come back here?"

"Is that what you call me for?"

"I remember you telling me you were sent here to do time."

"I was sent here to do time. You must be confusing me with somebody else. I've spoken with you on only one occasion, and that was to request a transfer."

"Oh, I guess you're right. Pardon me."

"That's okay. What did you want with me?"

"You will be seeing the parole board next Monday at ten."

"Thank you for telling me."

"Mr. Light will be there with you. Good luck."

"Thanks again."

I got up and walked out of his office. I was excited, and anxious for Monday to get here, but I didn't show it.

At ten the following Monday morning I was waiting to be called in to see the parole board. The first person I saw was Mr. Light.

"Good morning. I saw you were back, and that surprised me. How have you been?"

"I'm okay. How are you doing, Mr. Light?"

"I'm all right, Mr. Evans, Are you ready to go in?"

"Sure."

When we walked into the room the members of the panel were there: two men and one woman. The hearing was very brief.

One member of the panel greeted the two of us.

"Good morning, Mr. Evans, Mr. Light. How are you doing?"

I replied, "Good Morning. I'm doing fine."

Mr. Light said, "Good morning."

Then came the pronouncement from the board.

"Mr. Light, we have read the report that you submitted on behalf of Mr. Evans, and we have taken it into consideration.

"Mr. Evans, we have evaluated your case. I'm afraid you'll have to come back and see us in two years, we don't believe your attitude has changed."

I stood up said "Thank you."

As I turned and started walking toward the door, I noticed they had a curious look on their faces, as if they were expecting me to react in some way to what they had said.

The woman on the panel asked, "Mr. Evans, are you okay? Do you have something you'd like to say?"

"No, I'm fine."

As I exited the room, Mr. Light was right behind me.

"Evans, are you okay?"

"Yeah, I'm fine," I said, smiling. "Why?"

"Of all the years I've been sitting on the parole board, I have never seen anything like that. I have listened to all kinds of stories from inmates, many of them crying as they spoke. But you showed no emotion at all."

"Mr. Light, I cry all the time, you just don't see it. My reasons are just different. I'm innocent of this crime, and that's the God's truth. The whole business hurts so bad that I try not to think about it. If I did, I probably wouldn't have made it this far. It's a heavy burden to carry around. I have learned to deal with it as best I can."

"I have indeed witnessed that. You have really made a change in your life. You have a strong constitution. You deserve parole, and I indicated that to them."

"Thank you. I really appreciate that. Before, I had nothing to look forward to. Now I may be out in two years. Though, it doesn't erase the label that's been burned in my soul. That's something I will be taking to my grave, until then, all I have is hope and the will to get out of here and to be there for my son. Considering all time I've already served, two more years is nothing. I could do that in a barrel with the lid sealed. Besides, that will give me enough time to get myself together."

With that I walked away.

As I was going down the hall toward my cellblock I passed a few guys in the hallway. One of them said, "Hey, Shoes, how did you make out with the parole board?"

"Denied."

Actually, I felt pretty good. Now I had something to look forward to: a chance of getting out after two more years. That would be a whole lot better than serving a sentence of double life plus 15 years.

A few weeks later I received a certified letter from the parole board stating my parole was denied based on the grounds that they felt "my attitude had not changed." I immediately appealed that decision.

In the meantime I took a vocational course in small engine repair. I liked it, it was something that I thought might come in handy when I got out of prison.

The instructor, Mr. Benjamin, was a civilian. He had retired from the service and was now teaching this course. He was very informative and an effective educator. He was a tall man, well built, in his 50s, with gray hair. He had a patch over his right eye. Some of the guys in the class called him One-Eyed Jack. He took the time to help and encourage everybody. He offered a complete course that prepared you for the street — possibly even for a job, or for starting your own business.

We were given hands-on experience. Everyone had an engine to tear down and rebuild within a specified amount of time. Mr. Benjamin came over to me.

"Mr. Evans, you could be a skilled mechanic if you wanted. You finished ahead of the others, so how about if you give them a hand?"

"There's nothing difficult about it. They simply aren't mechanically inclined. You've already told them at least twice what needs to be done. If they haven't gotten it from what you taught them, what makes you think they'll get it from me? No disrespect, but I'm here to learn all I can, not to waste my time showing those guys what to do. They aren't serious about this course."

"I can tell you know what you're doing, but you're not putting enough into it. You're doing just enough to get by."

"You may be right about that."

One day I received a letter from the U.S. Patent Commissioner.

Congratulations! You are now an entrepreneur.

I was so excited! Elated, in fact! After several minutes went by, however, the thrill of it began to diminish as I started thinking about the difficulty I would have in marketing my invention. I wrote to several universities for help. After three or four weeks the University of Oregon responded. They did all the marketing for me, but they thought it would be best if I took care of the production myself.

I wanted so much to share the good news with someone. At first I could think of no one to share it with but Jackie. But she was gone now.

TRANSFER TO PETERSBURG

It had been a good while since I talked to anyone on the phone other than Jackie and it was my day to make a phone call. I thought of my sister Kim. I wanted to surprise her, so I called her.

"Hello."

"Hey, what's up?"

"Hey Bro, how are you doing? It's so good to hear your voice! When are you coming home?"

"I don't know."

"Willie was over here yesterday."

"Who was?"

"Willie. He was over here yesterday."

"Are you sure? I thought he was still locked up in Terre Haute."

"No, he's home. He's been coming over here a lot. Every time I turn around he's at my door. He's been coming around here for at least four months now."

"Why is he hanging around your house?"

"I don't think he has anywhere to go. For a while he was trying to hit on me, but I told him I wasn't interested. He backed off, but he kept coming around. I think he's looking for a place to stay, but I told him he couldn't stay here."

"The next time he comes around, ask him to send me a copy of his parole decision. I'd like to get that as soon as possible."

I could hardly believe what Kim had told me: that Willie was home. I found it hard to believe that he was out and I was still in, even though

I had done all the research and legal work. He could have at least written and told me he was out.

I stopped and told the guy in the cell next to mine about the conversation I had had with my sister.

"Man, you know how it is. After being locked up for so long, you forget about a lot of stuff."

"What? Just forget it, man. I don't know why I even mentioned it to you."

I went on to my cell.

About a week later I received a copy of Willie's parole decision. At that point I filed an extension to my appeal, and I wrote to my parole board and attached a copy of his parole decision. I also wrote a letter to the Judge, explaining what had happened, and I sent him copies of both our parole board decisions.

Meanwhile, there was a rumor going around that the Federal Correctional Institution in Petersburg, VA. were being converted to a minimum-security institution, and that they were transferring a lot of young inmates out of Petersburg and bringing in older inmates.

When the change was officially announced, I went to the library and read the guidelines to see if I would be eligible to go there.

"The guidelines stated Petersburg is being converted to a minimum-security correctional institution. To be eligible for placement there, an inmate must be within three years of his release date or his parole date."

I was now in that category, so I went to my caseworker and said, "Mr. Stonewall, I would like to be transferred to Petersburg."

"You're a violent criminal. We can't transfer you there, even though you fall within the guidelines."

"What? Please don't give me that nonsense. In the guidelines there's no mention that violent criminals are ineligible."

"I have the guidelines, and we have specific instructions on how we are to evaluate each individual."

I went back to the library, prepared a motion requesting a transfer to Petersburg on the basis of the stated guidelines, and filed it with the U.S. District Court in Pennsylvania. This was in December of 1981.

A few days later I was coming out of the cafeteria and saw the warden, George Adams, in the hallway. He had been my caseworker when I arrived at Lewisburg the first time. He was a nice guy, cool and calm. I walked over to him and said, "Hello, Mr. Adams. How are you doing?"

"Hello Mr. Evans. How have you been? Are you behaving yourself?"

"Yeah, but I'm having a little problem with my caseworker. I want to get transferred to Petersburg. I'm eligible, but he won't transfer me, so I had to file in the District Court."

"Have you had any infractions lately?"

"No."

"I suggest that you drop your case. Right now we have enough cases in court against the institution. But give me a few days, and I promise to look into it."

"Okay, but looking into it isn't the same as taking care of it."

He looked at me with a little smile and said, "I'll take care of it."

"Okay."

Two days later my caseworker called me to his office.

"Mr. Evans, I reconsidered your case, you will be leaving for Petersburg on the next bus out."

I thought to myself, He wants me to think he's helping me.

"Thanks."

"I want you to know that when you get out you'll have a clean record. You can start life all over again, but don't associate with Willie Gray. If you do and you get caught for something, you'll never see the streets again."

"What do you mean and what are you talking about?"

"Just remember that."

I got up and left.

RELEASE FROM PRISON

I had been at Petersburg for only about three or four months and I requested a furlough and I was denied. My caseworker in Lewisburg had placed a memo in my jacket saying: Dangerous, Keep in a Cell. I was prepared to go to court when I received a special delivery letter from the court. It was a copy of a court order addressed to the institution.

Release Kenzell Evans within 30 days.

Boy I was happy! I didn't say a word to anyone inside the institution, but I couldn't wait to call Jackie and tell her the news. When I dialed her number I got a recorded message: "The number you have dialed has been changed to an unpublished number." I hung up the phone and walked away.

A week later my new caseworker (the one in Petersburg) called me to his office.

"Mr. Evans, I've been going through your records. I'm going to see if I can get you out of here and into a halfway house. I've arranged for you to go to R & D. They'll be calling you soon."

I didn't tell him I had received a copy of the court order. He wanted me to think that he was trying to help me. He was young and arrogant and looked as if he had just gotten out of school.

I went back to my cell and made a vow to myself, that I would do everything in my power not to go back to my old ways, and to stay on the path that I was on.

I was released on September 12, 1982. They gave me $65 and took me to the bus station. The bus fare to Washington to D.C. was about $37. I purchased my ticket and sat down on the long bench in the waiting area and waited patiently for the bus to arrive.

While I was waiting I started pondering over the years I'd been confined in those unpleasant places. I felt like I had been barefooted, walking on broken glass the entire time, and came out without a scratch. Suddenly, I was interrupted by a young black woman in an Army uniform and the ticket man behind the counter. She was upset, crying, and pleading with him. She didn't have enough money to purchase a ticket and had to be back on base by a certain time or she would be charged with AWOL (being absent without leave). There were about five other people in the station, all of whom ignored her.

"How much more do you need?" I asked her.

"About twenty dollars."

"Here you go," I said as I handed her a twenty-dollar bill.

"Oh thank you, thank you. I'll give it back. What's your address? I'll send it to you."

"Don't worry about it. I'd rather that you just use it to help someone else who's in need."

"Please give me your address, so I can send it to you."

"You don't have to."

"Please, I can send it to you."

I wasn't really concerned about it, but she was persistent.

"All right, if that's what you want to do."

I gave her Nora's address, because I didn't have one.

When the bus came, I got on and sat near the back. I was so happy to be free that I forgot all about the incident with the Army woman. When I did recall it I thought to myself, I haven't been free for a full hour and I've already been suckered out of $20.

I just smiled, for that was the last thing on my mind.

The bus arrived at the Greyhound station in Washington around 12:40 p.m. How good it felt to be back! It had been about eleven years since I last set foot in D.C.

The first thing I noticed was that the station was still located in the same place, despite the fact that I remembered the guy in Lewisburg saying "Man, they've made so many changes in Washington that you aren't going to recognize it when you get out."

There were a few new buildings, and some renovation was going on, but the rest was the same. I definitely wasn't lost.

I remembered the caseworker telling me, "You have to report to the halfway house within 24 hours of your release."

That made me think of various stories I had heard from inmates when they were returned to prison for a violation such as not reporting on time, not returning to the halfway house on time, or breaking house rules. I thought the price they'd had to pay for such minor infractions was excessive, but I never said anything.

Considering how long I'd been locked up, I didn't want to take any chances. After getting off the bus, I briefly looked around and then started walking to the halfway house at Thirteenth and Clifton Streets, N.W. It felt so good to be free.

When I got there it was about 1:30 p.m. After checking in I met my counselor, a black guy.

"Hi, my name is Billy Moye. I'm going to be your counselor during your stay here."

"How you doing Mr. Moye, I'm Kenzell Evans."

"I can see that you and I are going to get along just fine."

"I hope so."

He was about my age, light skinned, tall, and slim. He was straightforward, an average guy, and worked part time at the halfway house. I felt comfortable with him.

"I see you've been gone for a while."

"I guess I have."

"And I see that you have a place to go and will be with us for only 60 days. That's good, man. A lot of these guys have nowhere to go, and most of them have three to six months to find a place to live. I think a lot of them end up wanting to go back to prison."

"Why do you say that?"

"You'll see."

"I'll take your word for it."

"One of the rules is that you must keep your room clean and your bed made up at all times—except when you're in it, of course. Also, everybody here is assigned to a detail around the house, unless you have an outside job, so I advise you to find a job as soon as you can. I'm going to put you in one of the better rooms, with a guy who has a job and keeps things clean."

He had one of the in-house orderlies give me bed linens and then showed me to my room.

"This *is* clean!"

"You can leave if you like, but you have to be in by 7:30 p.m."

"I think I'll hang around here and watch TV."

"That's fine if it's what you want to do, but you've got several hours until 7:30."

My son was the first thing that came to my mind but I didn't know where he was.

Since I hadn't told anybody I was getting out, I decided to go over to Nora's place. I took a cab to Southeast and told the driver that all I had was eight dollars.

"I'll take you only as far as I can for that much."

When we got to Fourth Street, S.E. he said, "This is as far as your money will take you."

I got out of the car and started walking. After two or three blocks I noticed a young woman hanging clothes on a clothesline. She was staring at me, and I kept looking at her as I continued to walk. She eventually leaned her head toward me and, with a smile on her face, started hollering my name: "Kenzell! Kenzell! Kenzell!"

It was my sister Paula!

"Paula! I didn't recognize you at first."

"Where did you come from?"

"I took a cab and was on my way to your mother's house. When my money ran out the driver dropped me off, just up the street. So I started walking."

"Why didn't you catch the bus?"

"I don't know the bus routes. Besides, I didn't think about taking a bus."

"How much did the cab driver charge you?"

"He charged me eight dollars to go from uptown to Fourth Street, S.E."

"He overcharged you."

"It's no big deal."

"I'm on my way over to Mama's now. You can ride with me. I want to see her face when you knock on her door."

"But you have some work to do."

"Oh, I can get this done later."

She stopped what she was doing, and we got into her car and drove to Nora's place.

"I have a daughter."

"Really, how old is she?"

"She's seven, but she thinks she's seventeen. She lives with Mama, who has spoiled her.

"Does Mama know you're coming?"

"No. Nobody knows I'm out."

When we walked in, Nora did show some emotion, so I apparently had caught her by surprise, but there wasn't a whole lot of excitement on her part.

Paula said, "This is my daughter, Jean. Jean, this is your Uncle Kenzell."

She was light skinned and a little on the chubby side.

"I know who he is."

"Hello Jean."

She walked back into the bedroom with the phone in her hand. She acted as if she was our age. Nora and Paula thought her behavior was cute and funny, and saw nothing wrong with it. I thought she was very disrespectful and showed no sign of home training.

Paula said, "The cab driver charged him eight dollars to go from uptown to Fourth Street, S.E.

"He knew you were new around here. You should have gotten the number on his car."

Paula and I had been at Nora's house for no more than ten minutes when someone knocked on the door. Paula went to the door and opened it. Low and behold, Willie was standing there, laughing. I was shocked to see him.

"Where did you come from, and how did you know I was here?"

He just laughed and said, "I'm always over here. It's easy to get around the city on the subway."

Nora and Paula didn't act as if there was anything unusual going on. They probably thought I had told Willie to meet me there.

"Come on. Let's go out to our old neighborhood, in Northeast."

I thought, Boy, he's moving fast. He popped up out of nowhere and already wants to go out to the old neighborhood.

"I just got here, and I'm still puzzled. How did you know I was here?"

"I told you I'm always in this area."

"You may always be in this area, but that doesn't mean you're always at this house."

At point I decided to back off, to avoid drawing any attention to Willie's showing up here. Somewhere I had read, "Sometimes it's best to keep quiet and play dumb, and you'll find out what you need to know. If you ask too many questions, you may end up learning nothing."

I was still puzzled, and I recalled what my case manager had told me about staying away from Willie. When we got outside I said, "I don't have any money, and I have to be back at the halfway house by 7:30."

I thought nothing else about it since he said okay, and we decided to walk out to Northeast since it was a nice day.

As we were walking away from the house I again asked him, "How did you know I was here?"

"You know how the word gets out."

I thought about what he said, but I hadn't told anybody I was coming home.

Willie went on to say, "Man, things have been hard since I got home, especially trying to find a job. I think we should get a place together."

"You must be out of your damn mind! You've been out for over six months and you still don't have a job? You've got to be crazy. We're not getting anything together."

I didn't mean to come on that strong. I was trying to be calm and didn't want him to become suspicious in any way, but he had pushed the wrong button.

Willie didn't say another word about sharing a place. He started talking about the people he had seen, and what they were doing and why. Things that was unimportant and totally irrelevant. As we walked through the old neighborhood, I saw a few guys I knew. They didn't appear to be particularly excited about seeing us, so I figured Willie must have been hanging out in that area. From the looks on their faces and the way they were dressed, I could see that they weren't doing very well and that they all had their share of problems.

"Do you always hang out like this, just wasting your time? I can understand why you haven't found a job."

"No, I thought you might want to come out here. I have been looking for a job."

"Shit, there's nothing out here that interests me."

"Not much has changed since we left. Jim, Mo, and Ronnie still hang out at Dave's Liquors, talking about old times."

At one point a guy walked up to us and said, "Man, it's hard out here. There are no jobs out here for a brother. Can you spare some change?"

"You came to the wrong place, bro," I replied.

"What about you, Willie?"

"I don't have any money. I'm broke, man."

I looked at them and thought, damn! He knows Willie.

I figured that Willie must have been doing nothing but hanging around here for some time now, possibly ever since he got out, because it was the only thing he had to show me.

It was getting late, about 5:45 p.m.

"I have to get back to the halfway house."

"I don't have any money."

"Before we came out here I told you I didn't have any money, but you didn't say that you didn't have any either. Man, fuck you. You got me wasting my time out here fucking with you."

I had to get back by 7:30 p.m. As I was trying to figure out what to do, I thought of Sheila. We had lived with her family for a short while after I first came to D.C. That was in this very neighborhood, in a house that had belonged to Sheila's grandmother. I went to that house, hoping Sheila still lived there.

To my surprise and wonder, she came to the door.

"Hello Sheila."

"Hi Kenzell, when did you come home?"

"I just got out this morning, and I have to get back to the halfway house by 7:30 p.m., but I don't have any money. I came out here with Willie, but he didn't let on until just a few minutes ago that he had no money either. Thank God I thought of you."

"He's not right. I always knew there was something not quite right when you got locked up with him. Besides, your mother knew you were innocent and didn't do a thing to help you. She got your brother a lawyer, and she knew *he* was guilty. My grandma used to tell her all the time, 'You shouldn't treat Kenzell like that. You should try to help him. Of all your kids, he's the only one trying to make something of himself.'"

"I hate to interrupt, but I don't have time to get into that right now. Could you possibly lend me six dollars to catch a cab, so I can get back on time? I promise I'll pay you back."

"I don't have that much. I have only some change."

She went in the house and came back with a handful of change.

"I have about $2.40. That'll be more than enough to get you back by bus."

"Thank you. However, I don't know anything about the bus routes or the schedules."

"Come on. I'll show you where to catch the bus. There should be one coming soon. It'll take you about 40 minutes to get there."

"Thanks a million, Sheila."

"Anytime Kenzell."

"Well, here comes the bus. I'll talk with you later. Thanks again."

I got on the bus and took a seat near the door and focused my attention on getting back to the halfway house on time. I thought to myself, Willie was trying to set me up to go back to prison.

The bus made pretty good time, but then it turned off onto H Street instead of going straight on Florida Avenue as I had expected. That's when I panicked. I got off the bus and started running. I ran all the way to the halfway house from the corner of H Street and Florida Avenue, N.E. I made it back on time and resolved not to take any chances like that again.

That night I met my roommate. He was about my age and very quiet. His name was Lewis.

"Man, I don't associate with these guys in here. They're not trying to do anything to improve their well being. They just sit around and shoot the bull. I'm so glad I found a job. I've been working for three months. I have just one more week here, and I can't wait to get out."

"How long did they give you to find a place of your own?"

"Six months. And I did find myself a place. You have to stay here until you find a job, and you might get blamed for a lot of the shit these guys do."

"I appreciate that, man. I've heard about some of the stuff they do. Is this your newspaper?"

"Yeah, here you can have it."

I went through the want ads and found something that interested me, but I had to go see my caseworker in the morning.

The next morning I got up and ate breakfast, and finished my assigned chores at the halfway house around 8:30 a.m. Then I ran downtown to see my parole officer, Mr. Green, since I had no money for bus fare or a cab. He was a small white man, shorter than I was. We introduced ourselves, and he explained the dos and don'ts. I could smell the alcohol on his breath as he spoke. After my meeting with him I ran back to the halfway house.

LIFE ON THE OUTSIDE

The next morning I was up and out of the house by six. I didn't eat breakfast, because I had planned to run to Mount Rainier, MD; to apply for a job. I wanted to be there early, when the place opened.

"When can you start?"

"I can start now."

"I'll start you at $11 an hour. The hours are 7 a.m. to 4 p.m., including an hour for lunch. I'll assign you to a crew, and I'll have one of the supervisors speak with you either this evening or tomorrow morning."

The job was with McCourtney & Sons Roofing Company. It was a small firm and hadn't been in business very long, but I could see that it was growing. They didn't mind that I was inexperienced. They were looking for manpower and were willing to provide on-the-job training, and I was willing to learn. Since I didn't yet have any money, I ran to and from work every day. That didn't bother me, because I was used to running.

After receiving my first paycheck I took a couple days off to get my driver's license. I paid Patrice to take me to the Department of Motor Vehicles, and she let me use her car to take the test. I also took the motorcycle test — only a written test was required for that — and passed both of them. She was surprised.

"I had to come back twice before I passed the test, and you just got home and passed it the first time."

"There was nothing to it. I've never forgotten how to drive."

I had been driving a car before any of them. Joe was the only one who had a license and was driving before I left. My neighbor had taught me how to ride a motorcycle. He had two and would let me ride one of them.

After that she didn't let me use her car unless I gave her some money.

The next day I asked Paula, "Can I use your car to go downtown to take care of some business?"

"No, you're not going to tear up my car."

"I want to go see about a job."

I had actually made an appointment with someone downtown to discuss my invention, but I couldn't tell Paula that. She wouldn't have understood what I was talking about.

"Not with my car."

I asked Nora if I could use her car, and she too said no.

I called and rescheduled my appointment, and then caught the bus to downtown. While I was there I went to the courthouse.

"Could you tell me where I need to go to file for a divorce?"

"You come right here."

"You can do it yourself. You have to be separated for at least six months, and both parties have to consent. Basically, all you need to do is fill out this form. The court cost is $45. It should take no more than 30 days if both parties consent."

"May I take one of these forms?"

"Sure."

When I got back to the halfway house I filled out the form, but I couldn't complete it because I didn't know Margie's address.

I sat there in my room thinking about all years I been gone without Nora being in my life, I never missed her or thought about her for that matter. I'm not mad at her, I don't hate her. The relationship between us has always been an up hill battle for me, but no sooner than I was released, the first place I went was to her place after checking in at the halfway house.

I know she don't care, but I had to ask myself, why did I go over to her place when I got out, and why am I trying to throwing myself on her. The only honest answer I could come up with was—I wanted to be accepted.

The first free weekend I had, I went to Pennsylvania to visit my cousin Dan and his wife Pat. When Pat opened the door her eyes lit up, "Where did you come from? When did you get out?"

"I came home two weeks ago," I said, smiling.

"Come on in. Dan! Dan! Come here! Look who's here!"

"How you been Pat?"

"I've been okay Kenzell. I'm glad you're out, we kept you in our prayers."

Dan came running down the stairs. "What is it? What is it?" he asked. Then he looked up and saw me. A big smile appeared on his face.

"Hey, when did you come home? I'm very happy to see you, Kenzell."

"I got out about two weeks ago. First, I want to thank both of you for coming to see me. You don't know how much it has changed me. Thank you again."

"You're welcome," said Pat.

"I'm glad it worked out for you," added Dan. "We've kept you in our prayers. Thanks for coming to see us. Would you like something to eat? Can I get you something? Make yourself at home."

"I'm okay. I can't stay long, because I'm living in a halfway house and I have to get back."

"How did you get here?"

"I came by bus and then took a cab from the bus station."

"You move fast."

"I know you and Dan has a lot to talk about, so I'm going to go upstairs and let you guys talk."

"You take care, Pat."

"You take care of yourself, Kenzell."

"I'm so happy to see you, man. You were pretty hard on us when we went up to see you. I was telling Pat that that place had changed you, because you didn't seem to care about things to the extent that you had before you were locked up."

"Dan, there's a lot you don't know about me. I didn't choose this life I'm living, but I know I have to deal with it.

"Dan, I was railroaded. I'm out, but I didn't clear my name and that's something that will always be on my mind, it has become my secret, and I have to live with that thought everyday of my life. I guess I should have concentrated on clearing my name instead of concentrating on getting out. That's what happens when you put the wagon in front of the horse.

"At any rate, now that I'm out I can't play catch up and I can't put my life on hold. I have to do what I know best—survive. You would have to be in my shoes to understand what I'm talking about."

"I guess you're right. You've evidently handled it well. I don't know what I would've done in your situation."

"You do what you have to do."

"Have you seen your son yet?"

"No. I don't know where he's living, but I'll find him and I'll get him.

I thought about my son a lot over the years I was away. One day I woke up and realized he needs me, and from that day I was determinate to get myself out. I didn't want my son to go through what I gone through. He has been the driving force in my life for getting out.

"What happened with you and Jackie?"

"She met this guy from England, and I faded away. She's a beautiful person, and I don't feel that he deserves her, but who am I to say that?"

"I understand where you're coming from."

"Do you?"

"Yeah, Jackie was all right," he said, smiling.

"I know she was."

"You are cold, Kenzell."

"I was trying to be realistic, Dan."

"Now that you're out, what do you plan to do?"

"Well, I came up with an invention when I was in Lewisburg, and I'm going to see if I can get it off the ground, but what I really need is money."

"You came up with an invention? Do you have a patent on it?"

"Sure."

"Kenzell, that's great! I wish I could invent something."

"You can, but it's not all that simple. Besides, I haven't had any luck with it so far. It's definitely not what I thought it would be. What are you doing?"

"I'm not doing anything right now. I spend a lot of time in church."

"How about Pat?"

"She's a librarian, but I don't want my wife to work."

"I see. Oh, I have to get going and catch my bus."

"Okay Kenzell, I'm glad you came to see us."

"I'll try to get here and see y'all again."

When I went to work the following Monday I asked the supervisor, "Do you mind if I work on the ground? I don't care much for heights."

"That's fine with me if it's what you want. You realize that there will be a difference in pay, don't you?"

"That's okay with me."

One of the guys working on the roof overheard our conversation and said, "You've got to be crazy! Working on the roof pays more than working on the ground."

I just smiled at him.

It was a hot afternoon, and we were starting work on a job downtown,

at a new Roy Rogers restaurant. Two guys were hauling buckets of hot tar up the ladder to the roof when one of them suddenly slipped and spilled tar on both of them. He dropped the bucket, and both of them fell off the ladder and down to the ground, hollering and screaming at the top of their lungs, like cats. The tar had peeled the skin off their bodies, especially their hands and arms, and even off the face of one of them. It had gone right through their clothes.

People were standing by, watching in horror. There was nothing anyone could do but wait for the ambulance to come. Whenever a towel or blanket was draped over either of the guys, their skin came right off, which prompted some of the onlookers to holler "Don't touch them!" Eventually, the ambulance came and took them away.

Shortly thereafter I quit that job and found another, this time as an educational consultant, which was nothing more than a fancy title for a door-to-door encyclopedia salesman. This turned out to be a big mistake. I never made any sales. It gave me a lot of free time away from the halfway house, but I wasn't making any money. I kept looking for another job in the meantime.

One day Mr. Moye said to me, "We have to move some guys out of here. We need beds for the new people coming in. Your name is on the list of those that have to leave. Do you have a place to go?"

"Yeah, I think so."

"I'll need the address of your place of residence."

"Sure."

I called Nora.

"Hello."

"Hi. How are you?"

"I'm all right."

"I just finished talking to my counselor. He said they have to move people out of the halfway house to make room for new people. I'm one of the ones that have to leave. I gave them your address. I hope that's all right."

"How much money are you making? You'll have to pay rent. You can't stay here for nothing."

That reminded me of how she had treated me when I was younger and living with her. She evidently hadn't changed one bit.

"I know."

I moved out of the halfway house and went back to living with Nora. Joe was rarely there. And when he was, he stayed in the back bedroom with the door closed. If I spoke to him, he didn't respond. I didn't let that bother me, because that's how he'd always been, and how he and Nora had raised their other kids. They spoke to me only when they wanted something.

I had been saving my money from the roofing job, and I agreed to give Nora $50 a week.

"How much money are you making a week?"

"About $90, but they don't need me all the time. Meanwhile, I'm looking for another job."

"I hope you succeed, because $50 a week isn't enough for rent. You'll have to do better than this."

I stayed there as little as possible, usually only two or three nights a week, because the place was full of negativity. Being there with them, around them allowed old memories of when I was young to surface. They behaved as if I had never gone anywhere. They hadn't changed. On other nights I stayed at a motel, but I had to use Nora's address to make it look legit to my caseworker. I knew I wouldn't be staying at her place for long. Being away from them gave my mind serenity and peace.

RECONNECTING WITH MY SON

One evening when I was at Nora's, somebody knocked on the door. I answered it and saw that it was Barbara, Margie's sister. I stepped outside to talk to her. I figured Willie had told her I was home.

"Yeah, what is it?"

"Hi Kenzell, we want to take you to dinner."

"Who is 'we'?"

"Margie and I want to take you to dinner. She's in the car."

"I haven't seen or heard from her in over ten years, and now she wants to take me to dinner? Y'all don't have to do that, I'm okay. I'm not hungry either, and y'all are wasting my time."

I walked to the car and said to Margie, "Where is Kenzell Junior?"

"Hi. He'll be glad to see you. We live at—I'll write the address and phone number down for you."

"I'll be over there to see him."

"I'll let him know."

I turned and started walking back toward the house.

"Kenzell, you don't have to be like that. Margie wants to see you. Everybody makes mistakes."

I just looked at her.

"See you later."

As I walked back to the house I thought to myself, I can finish filling out that divorce form now and file it, then get my son.

When I got inside, Nora asked, "Who was that?"

"I don't know. They were looking for somebody named Billy."

"You had to go outside to tell them that?"

"They were lost and wanted directions."

"Where are you when you're not here?"

"Oh, I'm at the homes of friends of mine, playing cards."

"Don't be bringing drugs in here."

"I don't mess with drugs."

The following morning I reached for the telephone.

"Get off my phone."

I was shocked.

"I'm trying to take care of some business."

"You're not using my phone. You'll have to go elsewhere to make your calls."

"I'm trying to contact a company that deals with inventions. I have a patent."

"I don't care what you have. You're not using my phone."

Jean walked toward me with a smile on her face and picked up the phone. She took the phone into the room with her and started talking to her friend. Nora didn't reprimand her for using the phone. I didn't say a word, and I never again touched Nora's phone. I went to the phone booth and made my calls.

Then I called my son.

"Hello."

I didn't recognize the voice. It sounded like that of a little girl.

"May I speak to Kenzell?"

"Just a minute."

About two minutes later he came to the phone.

"Hello."

"Hey, little man, how are you doing?"

"I'm okay."

"Do you know who you're talking to?"

"No."

"This is your dad."

"This is my daddy?"

"That's right. I'm home now, and I'm coming to get you tomorrow."

"You are?"

"I'll pick you up after school."

"Okay."

"See you tomorrow."

Once I left the phone booth and started walking up the street, I saw a car approaching from the opposite direction. The car pulled over to the curb, and the driver called out to me: "Hey Shoes! Shoes! What's up?"

I stopped and looked, but I couldn't make out who it was. The guy got out of the car and said, "What's happening, man?"

I started smiling and thought to myself, it's Wayne.

"What's up, man?"

We walked toward each other and embraced.

"It's good to see you, man."

"It's good to see you too."

"Do you have time to talk?"

"Sure. There's nothing in particular that I have to do today."

"Come on. Let's go to a place where we can sit down and have a glass of wine."

We got into his car, and he drove to a Red Lobster in Virginia.

"How long have you been home?"

"About two months. I got out of the halfway house a couple weeks ago."

"What are you doing?"

"I'm finding my way right now. I had a roofing job for a while, but that wasn't my thing. I thought about going back to school to become a paralegal, but I was concerned that that might bore me."

"I came up with an invention after you left Lewisburg."

"What kind of invention?"

"It is an exercise bar."

"Do you have a patent?"

"Yeah, but it's not going very well. I don't have the resources to pursue it. Everyone I've contacted about it expects me to put up $1,500, or more and if I had it I wouldn't pay them for something I can do myself."

"I can see you getting into some kind of business. By the way, how is Jackie? Do y'all still talk?"

"No, that ended."

"What about Jim?"

"I haven't thought about him."

"How is your son? Have you seen him?"

"Not yet, but I just now spoke with him. I told him I'd see him tomorrow. He sounded enthused but curious."

"Well, you can understand that. After all, he was only three when you last saw him. It's been a long time for both of y'all. You'll need time to re-establish your relationship with him."

"I'm in the process of filing for divorce and I'm going to try to get custody of him."

"I wish you luck."

"What's going on with you? How is your family?"

"I've been divorced and remarried. I've relocated too. I live and work in Pennsylvania now. You'll have to come up and visit sometime."

"I just might do that if you give me your address and phone number."

"Sure. I have my kids with me too. Here you go. Can I get your address and phone number?"

"Sure, that's my mother's address. I don't have a phone."

"My employer gave me a week to finish up my business here, but I wrapped it all up this morning. I have a few days left. Would you like to go to Atlantic City?"

"Man, I can't go to Atlantic City. I don't have any money, and I wouldn't go up there just to watch other people gamble."

He reached into his pocket, pulled out $500, and handed it to me.

"What's your excuse now?"

"What's behind this?"

He laughed.

"Nothing, you said you have no money. Man, you know me better than that. Just accept it as a blessing. If you don't spend it all in Atlantic City or don't want it, you can pass it on to someone else as a blessing."

"You'll get it back. I have to see my parole officer tomorrow morning, and I told my son I would pick him up after school tomorrow. Wouldn't it take you out of your way to get me back on time for those things?"

"No. Come on man. I'd have you back on time, but if you're reluctant we won't go. I don't want to get you in trouble."

"When do you want to leave?"

"We can go now."

As he drove to Atlantic City he said, "Man, I've often thought about you since I got out. I didn't think you'd ever be released, for they were denying every motion you filed. I'm glad you proved me wrong."

"Yeah, the Judge was being an ass, denying everything I filed. Instead of appealing them, I let them go. To this day I regret not appealing. He denied the last motion I filed, and I appealed it, and the Appeals Court reversed it. That's how I got out."

"I told you I'd get out, but I didn't clear my name. The thought of that still hangs over my head, and it bothers me when I think about it."

"I'm sorry for bringing it up. But you dealt with it as if it were nothing. I don't think I could've handled that."

"Man, I'm so glad you're out. I tell my wife about you all the time. You've got to meet her one day."

"I'd love to meet her, but I have to get myself together first."

When we got to Atlantic City, Wayne said, "Come on. Let's go over here to the dollar machines."

"Where do I put my money for this machine?"

"Right here, put in twenty dollars and play the max."

"Enjoy yourself, and good luck."

I started pulling the arm. After putting in two more twenty-dollar bills, I saw a red seven and a pair of bonus stars pop up, and the machine started spewing out coins. Wayne heard the noise and came over.

"That's all right! It paid off."

"It sure did! Here, take half of this."

"No, just enjoy yourself."

The machine kept paying off. I had won enough coins to fill three buckets, worth a total of $1,800. I went back to the same machine and won $400 more. From there I went to another machine and won $900, and I still had $180 left of the money Wayne had given me.

Wayne had won $600.

"I guess my luck is fading."

"It's getting late. Perhaps we should leave."

Handing him $600 I said, "Here's your money back."

"No, keep it. I'm okay."

"Thanks a lot. By the way, there's no need for you to take me back. I can catch a bus to D.C."

"I'll take you back."

"Man, you've done enough already, and I appreciate everything. I may look small, but I'm a big boy. I know how to get home."

"I'll take you to the bus station."

We got into the car, and Wayne drove only about two blocks before I saw the station.

"Damn! The bus station is right here. I could've walked."

We didn't know it was this close.

"Okay man, call me."

"I will, you take care Wayne."

"You too Shoes."

I went into the station to find out when the next bus would be leaving for Washington. The attendant said, "The next bus leaves at 3 a.m."

"What about the next one after that?"

"That one departs at 6:00 a.m."

I turned around and went back to the casino and picked up $680 more. However, I felt that the machines weren't paying as well as they had earlier, so I left and went back to the bus station and waited.

When I got back to D.C., I walked a few blocks to see my parole officer, and in the afternoon I caught a cab and went to pick up my son at school. I was happy to see him, but he was quiet, as if he didn't quite know what to say. I did most of the talking. The first thing I noticed was the clothing he was wearing.

"What grade are you in now?"

"I'm a freshman in high school."

"How are you doing in school? Do you play any sports?"

"I'm doing fine. I like basketball, but I don't have a good pair of basketball shoes."

"Let's go to the store and get the things you need."

We caught a cab and went to the mall.

When we got there I told him, "Get whatever shoes you want."

"Can I get these shoes here?"

"Yeah, if that's what you want. You'll need a pair of dress shoes too."

"Pick out some clothes you like."

"I like this shirt."

"Man, you're in high school now. Get yourself four or five outfits, and some socks and underwear. When you get home, take off this stuff you have on and put it in the trash."

"Mom won't like that."

"Don't you worry about that, if she complains, you tell her I told you to throw it in the trash."

He just looked at me.

"That's right. Tell her what I said. Do you have a coat, a good coat?"

"No."

"Get yourself a good coat. Better yet, get yourself two coats: a full-length coat and a short jacket. Don't worry about me. Just get what you need, Junior. Now that I'm home, things are going to be different. Just concentrate on your schoolwork."

"Okay Dad."

"Since you're in high school now, I hope this will take some of the pressure off."

"It sure will," he said, smiling.

"I'm glad to be with you man."

"I'm glad you're here too."

"It's getting late. Is there anything else you need?"

"No. This is a lot as it is."

"I don't have a place of my own right now, but I will, and then you can come live with me if you like."

"I'd like that."

"Give me a little time."

"Okay, I will."

"I don't have a phone either, but we'll be talking, and you take care."

"I will. Thanks, Dad."

RON: FRIEND AND BUSINESS PARTNER

The next day I went to a car auction that I been hearing so much about, a place where I figured I could get a good deal. I came out with a white 1979 Cadillac Eldorado, which I got for $1,300. When I drove it I noticed it needed new brakes. I remembered how to put brake shoes on, but I had no tools. Joe knew something about cars, so I went to see him.

"Would you be willing to put brakes on my car? I'll pay you."

"I don't work on cars anymore, but I know somebody who would do it for you."

Just two days prior I had seen him putting brakes on somebody else's car, right out in front of the house, but I kept my mouth shut about it.

Joe called the friend, a guy by the name of John, and I took my car over to John's house. He proceeded to remove one of the wheels.

"You need rotors and brake pads. Altogether, the job will cost you about $300."

"Man, you must be out of your damned mind! Put that wheel back on my car."

As he was putting the wheel back on he said, "It's possible that I could get it done a little cheaper. Let me call my parts store. I don't know what I was thinking. My mind was on something else."

"Just put the wheel back on. I didn't come out here to have you bullshit me. All you've done is waste my time."

"Let me call another store."

He didn't want me to leave.

I got into my car and drove off. I just knew that Joe had something to do with this.

I drove through my old neighborhood and saw a guy I knew by the name of Bobby. He had been working on cars for as long as I could remember. They used to refer to him as the grease monkey of the neighborhood. He was a good mechanic.

"Hey Bobby, what's going on?"

"Hey Kenzell, when you come home?"

"About two months ago. Do you still work on cars?"

"Yeah, you got some work for me?"

"My car needs rotors and brakes."

"That's no problem. How soon you want it done?"

"Now, if you can."

"Pull into the yard, and let me jack it up so I can see what you need."

"You don't need rotors. They're fine, and your rear brakes are okay. All you need is pads for the front. The ones that on it now are shot. Let's go over to Pep Boys and get them. The pads should cost no more than ten dollars. Give me twenty five dollars, and I'll knock it right out."

"You got it."

"These tires you got on here are no good. The treads are practically gone. That's dangerous, man. I'm going to give you the tires off that Cadillac over there. It belonged to my father, and he no longer wants it. I been taking parts off of it, and the tires are the only thing left that's any good."

"Are you sure he won't mind?"

"It's okay. You can have the tires. I'm just going to switch them with the tires from your car so my dad's Cadillac won't be sitting on the ground."

"Thanks, Bobby."

He finished everything in about two hours. I took another $50.out of my pocket and handed it to him.

"Thanks man, you sure made my day."

When I got back to Nora's place and walked in, everybody fell silent. Then Jean broke the silence.

"Did you get your car fixed?"

I didn't answer her.

It looked as though Joe wanted to say something but couldn't get it out of his mouth.

Nora said, "Why didn't you let John do your brakes?"

"He said he had something else to do."

"He said you left."

"He told me to come back next week."

"Stop lying. Where did you get money to buy a Cadillac anyhow?"

Without saying a word I got up and left.

I drove to the park, and thought about all the money I had saved. I was sorry I had asked Joe. I had done that only because I thought he could get it done cheaper. I could've gone to a dealer and gotten it done for less than what his friend was going to charge me.

I don't even know why I bought a Cadillac. It was a damned gas guzzler, an expensive piece of junk. I didn't need anything like that. My mind must have been back in the penitentiary, with all those stories the other guys were forever telling about their Cadillac. I evidently wasn't thinking when I bought it. I should have gotten a smaller car but it was the only thing left worth getting.

The very next day I ran into my old friend Ron. I was glad to see him, and I gathered that the feeling was mutual.

"How is Margie and Junior? Y'all still together?"

"No, we're not. She came to see me three times when I was in Baltimore. She stayed for all of 15 minutes each time. That was eleven years ago. Barbara had the audacity to bring her around to my mother's house one night last week, talking about the two of them taking me to dinner."

"You seen your son?"

"Yes, I have. In fact, I saw him just the other day. He's confused. He's been told a bunch of lies, and he thinks everybody is kin to him. He's been neglected, but he's going to be all right. I'm in the process of getting a divorce, and I'm going to try to get custody of him."

"I'm sorry to hear that, man. I wish you luck with it. I have three kids now. They live with their mother. She and I didn't get along. Getting involved with her was the biggest mistake of my life, but I love my kids. I have them with me every chance I get. You'll have a chance to meet them, and I hope we'll all get to see Junior"

"What you been doing?"

"Nothing right now, I just got out of the halfway house and I'm staying with my mother."

"You don't need to stay there. I live alone in a three-bedroom townhouse in Maryland. You can stay with me until you get yourself together."

"Thanks, but I don't want to impose on you."

"You won't be imposing on me. Think about it."

"I'll do that."

"In fact, I'm going home right now. Why don't you follow me? Then you'll know where I live."

When we got to his house he said, "Come on in."

"You have a nice place here, Ron."

"Thanks man. Would you like something to eat or drink? I have some wine."

"I'm not hungry, but I wouldn't mind having a glass of wine."

"Okay, it's coming right up. Well, what do you think? Would you like to move in with me?"

"Give me a few days to get my things together."

I went back to Nora's house and I said, "Thanks for letting me stay here. I'll be moving out within the next few days."

"Don't forget to pay your rent for this week."

"This week has just started, and I was here for only one day last week."

"I don't care. I want my money. You can't stay here for nothing."

"Trust me. I'm well aware of that. I'm also aware that nobody else in this place has to pay rent."

I didn't go straight to Ron's house. Over the next two days I looked for a job and slept in my car. Then I moved in with Ron. While living with him I got up early every morning and ran for 30 minutes. I followed that up with 30 minutes of other exercises, just as I had done when I was in the penitentiary.

I filed for divorce, and I spent a lot of time with my son. I was happy to be with him, and he was just as happy as I was. He had been in bad shape mentally when I got out. It really hurt me to see him in that condition. He knew who he was, and that was about it. I felt sorry for him, because I had been there myself. All I could do was pray and be patient with him.

"Aunt Daisy and Uncle Frank go to the movies on Wednesdays. Can I go with them?"

"Junior, those people are no kin to you. They're just friends of your mother's."

"I've stayed with them and played with my cousins."

"They are no kin to you. Stop referring to them as your aunt, your uncle, and your cousins."

I was so angry that I took every opportunity I got to convince my son that those folks were no kin to him. Besides that, the lack of proper attention from his mother was obvious. I thanked God for letting me get to him when I did. He stayed with me most of the time when he wasn't in school.

I didn't get a chance to see Ron very much during the week. Most nights I was asleep by the time he got home from work, and I was already out and running by the time he got up for work in the morning. It was mainly on weekends that we spent time together, along with our kids. Junior got along well with Ron's kids. They never wanted to go home to their mother. Ron always had to calm them down before taking them home.

"Man, I go through this every time they're here."

"Why don't you try to get full custody?"

"Believe me, I've tried. The schedule I have doesn't allow me to spend much time with them. I would have to deal with their mother or find somebody to run them around, because they go to different schools. I'm not able to do that. Your son is older. You don't have to worry about that with him. My son Ron doesn't know how to keep his mouth shut, so I have to take off about twice a week to go to his school and deal with his latest disciplinary infraction."

While running one morning, I passed a man who was bent over his lawnmower, trying to get it to run. He was of medium size and looked to be in his 50s. I stopped and asked, "Do you need some help?"

"Yeah, I could use some. I don't know what I'm doing."

"It looks as if you have dirt in your carburetor."

"Where's the carburetor?"

"Do you have a Phillips head screwdriver?"

"Yeah, let me get one."

He left and came back with a screwdriver.

"Let me take a look."

I took off the carburetor, cleaned it, and put it back on. Then the lawnmower started right up.

"Damn, that was fast! I figured I'd have to take it to a repair shop, and I had no idea what it would cost me. My name is Roger Clay. How much do I owe you?"

"My name is Evans. You don't owe me a thing."

"I really appreciate it. You should go into the lawnmower repair business. I work at the landfill, and people are always throwing mowers away instead of having them fixed."

"Can you get them for me?"

"Yeah, they're just sitting out there."

"I tell you what: If you can get mowers for me, I'll fix them and you can sell them. We can split the profits."

"It's a deal! I'm off today and tomorrow, but I'll have some mowers here for you by Thursday afternoon."

"Okay, but first let me talk it over with my partner. I also need to get some tools."

"Let me know."

I continued with my morning run and started thinking about the conversation I had just had. The more I thought about it, the more excited I became.

That night I stayed up late enough to talk to Ron when he got home from work.

"While I was out running this morning I met a man who lives about five blocks from here. He couldn't get his lawnmower to run, so I stopped and fixed it for him."

"You know something about lawnmowers?"

"Yeah, I took a course in small engine repair while I was in prison, and I had fooled around with cars even before my incarceration. Hell, you should know. I fixed that raggedy-ass car you had."

"Oh, I remember."

"Anyway, this guy and I got to talking. His name is Roger Clay. He said he works at the landfill, where he can get lots of lawnmowers that people have thrown away. I told him that if he could get them, I would fix them and he could sell them, and we could split the profits. He agreed to that. I told him I needed a little time to talk it over with my partner."

"I'm with you. What you need?"

"Do you have any tools?"

"I have a few, and what I don't have we can buy."

"What I need shouldn't cost that much. You and I could embark on a business partnership."

"I can't quit my job just like that."

"I don't expect you to quit."

"I can do the paperwork and open up a business account at the bank."

The next day Ron said, "The account is set up in such a way that either of us alone can withdraw no more than $20. Both our signatures are required for withdrawals in amounts larger than that."

We went to Sears and got the tools I needed, and that Thursday I went over to see Mr. Clay.

"Hey, how are you doing? I was able to get only three mowers today. Do you want riding mowers too?"

"Sure, if you can resell them."

"Don't worry about that. I can easily get rid of them. I have a friend who has a truck, and he can get me about ten or more."

"Okay, but do you have enough space for them?"

"Come on back and take a look at the size of my backyard. I'm reminded of that every time I mow my lawn."

"The first riding lawnmower you bring me you can keep for your own use — after I fix it, of course."

That evening I fixed the three mowers he had brought home. The next day he sold them for $75 to $100 each and brought home four more for me. He had put word out to his family, friends, and neighbors that he was repairing lawnmowers. People started coming to his house and leaving their lawnmower to be repaired. As fast as the mowers were brought to him, I got them fixed.

As time went on, Mr. Clay's backyard began to look like a lawnmower graveyard and I started to fall behind in repairing them. I had started a lawn service in the meantime, and I used some of the mowers for that. Early in the morning I would take the lawnmowers, together with other tools I needed, and load them into the trunk of my car. For hired help I either drove to certain liquor stores early in the morning and got some guys together, or went downtown and got a crew from Manpower, where there would be guys lined up as early as 6 a.m. looking for work.

I stayed busy. I was out by 4:30 a.m. every morning to go for my run and get my exercise. I would try to finish up the lawn work by noon, and then I'd go to Mr. Clay's house to get some mowers to fix. I was getting home somewhere between 7:30 and 8:00 p.m. every night.

I was busy for seven months straight. People were constantly calling, and I couldn't keep up. I was working seven days a week and had no time for anything else. Ron helped out as much as he could and took off more days than he should have. His boss started calling, wanting to know why he hadn't shown up for work.

DIVORCE AND CUSTODY

I received a second letter from the court in regard to my divorce. I had missed the first hearing, and I didn't want to miss another one. When I went to court the Judge asked, "So you are Mr. Kenzell Evans?"

"Yes, I am."

"I thought your name looked familiar. If I remember correctly, you were at Lewisburg. I was an attorney back then, and I was representing your wife. She'd had another child, who she claimed was yours. I sent you an affidavit to sign, but I later figured out that her claim was false, so I had the case dismissed."

"When I got that affidavit, I had no idea what you were referring to. I knew I hadn't sired a child while I was locked up. In fact, I was hoping you would subpoena me. A change of scenery would have been good for me around that time."

"She had me believing her story for a while, but I caught on to her little scheme. Mr. Evans, I wish every man would step up and take responsibility for his children. Well, enough on that. What brings you here today?"

"All I want is a divorce and custody of my son."

"Do you want child support?"

"No."

"I'm granting you a divorce and custody of your child, Kenzell Evans, Jr. If you change your mind about child support, just come back and see me. I wish you the best."

"Thank you."

While I was out running the following morning I thought about what had transpired in court, especially about the Judge asking me if I wanted child support. If Margie had meant any good, she wouldn't have abandoned our son, and she wouldn't have had the nerve to have even more kids and then not raise *them* properly either. She once said she wanted more kids, and she got them.

Shortly after I got back to the house it started raining. I saw that it was coming down hard, so I decided to stay home and get some rest. By the time I got up it had diminished to a light drizzle, so I decided to walk down to the neighborhood store and pick up a few things. While I was there I bumped into Mr. Clay.

"Hey, Evans, I was going to tell you when you came over."

"Tell me what?"

"I won't be getting you any more lawnmowers. My supervisor has ordered me to stop."

"I was going to give it up anyway. I'm burned out. As the old saying goes, all good things must come to an end."

"I had never thought of it like that, especially since things were going so well. I guess you're right, but I had expected to continue bringing in that extra money. I just bought another car. What are we going to do now?"

"I don't know. I'll see you tomorrow."

"All right. You take care."

Truth be told, I didn't care. I was tired of it all.

When Ron came home he said, "Man, I have to pick the kids up early. Their mother has lost her job, and now she and the kids have nowhere to go."

"They can come here. I'll find a place of my own."

"You don't have to go anywhere."

"You can't deprive your kids of a place to live, regardless of how you feel about their mother. Let them come here. I'll be okay. I never intended to make this my permanent home. I have to get a place of my own."

"I guess you're right, but their mother argues all the time, especially around the kids, and I don't like that."

"That's something you'll have to work out with her. And if she doesn't listen, just ignore her. Who knows? She might learn something from it. At least give it a try. It wasn't all that bad when y'all had those kids, was it?"

"I do like her."

"Well, it's none of my business, but y'all didn't have just one child. Y'all had three, and they're not triplets. I've come to believe there's a reason for everything that happens in life. Put yourself in my shoes. I'm still trying to figure out why I went to jail for something I knew nothing about. If I were to dwell on that, I'd go crazy. You don't have a problem, just a decision that needs to be made, and a fairly simple one at that.

"I'll start looking for a place. I don't want to feel as if I'm taking advantage of a good thing, and I don't want to allow myself to get too comfortable here. I'd like to thank you from the bottom of my heart for letting me stay here, Ron. You have helped me more than you'll ever know. Thanks a million for everything.

"I'm ready for a change. I'm exhausted from what I've been doing: going out at 4:30 a.m. every morning and getting a crew together, transporting them to the work sites, hauling tools around in my car, repairing lawnmowers in the evenings, and not getting finished until 7:30 or 8:00 p.m. When I get here at night I'm so tired that I often just jump into the shower and go straight to bed, without even bothering to eat."

"I've been trying to tell you that you need to *take* some time for yourself. You've been working like an automaton. Whenever I told you to stop and take a break, you said you had to do this, that, or the other thing. I knew you were tired, but you wouldn't stop."

"I couldn't stop then, because I was too busy. I was getting a lot of calls. I never had a chance to spend any of the money I was earning, other than for the few tools we purchased."

Ron said, "Man, you wouldn't believe how much we have in the bank."

"To tell you the truth, I have no idea. I haven't had time to think about that. Now I can, however, for things have slowed down. Besides, Mr. Clay said he can't get any more lawnmowers, so I've decided to call it quits. That's hard work."

"I kept telling you it was hard work."

"I know. I knew what I was getting myself into, and that's why I didn't complain. Now that things have slowed down, I can get out. I have just one job to finish up."

I was working on that last job when a woman who was walking down the street approached me.

"Who does this car belong to? I love that body style."

"You can have it for $1,500."

"Are you serious? What year is it?"

"It's a 1979 model. Give me $1,500, and I'll sign over the title to you."

"Are you serious? What's wrong with it?"

"There's nothing wrong with it. I just don't want it anymore."

"Can I get your phone number? I want to talk to my husband about this, and I'll call you tonight."

"Here's my number," I said as I handed her a slip of paper.

The woman called me that night, and I sold her the car.

I was glad to get rid of that gas guzzler. The gas alone had cost me about five dollars to go ten miles. I was glad the jobs weren't that far away.

I was surprised to learn that Ron and I had saved over $65,000. We had far more than I would have guessed. We sold all the tools and divided everything up evenly. Despite having all that money, however, I didn't give my patent much thought. I just concentrated on getting an apartment for my son and me.

I bought myself a used MGB, and I moved into an apartment and furnished it.

Ron's girlfriend and their kids moved in with him, and shortly thereafter she became pregnant with their fourth child. They later got married.

Ron and I were still friends, and we kept in touch.

MY OWN BUSINESS

It was a Sunday afternoon I was watching a basketball game and reading the want ads in the newspaper when somebody knocked on the door. To my surprise, it was Sean.

"Hey, how you know I was here? Come on in."

"Mama said you had moved. I saw a friend of yours, and he gave me your address. This is a nice place you have here. How are you doing?"

"Thanks. I'm doing fine. I started a lawn service, but I had to let that go. It was wearing me out."

The look on his face gave me the impression that he either didn't care or didn't believe me.

"How long have you been living here?"

"That's not important. Is that what you came here to find out?"

"No. What are you doing now?"

"What are you doing?"

"I live and work in Pennsylvania, not far from Dan."

"Why are you asking me all these questions? Are you a reporter?"

"No."

"Then stop acting like one. I'm looking for something else to do. I was just looking through the want ads. I noticed there are jobs available for couriers. What is a courier?"

"Couriers are guys who ride bicycles around the city delivering packages."

"Oh. Well, I'm not interested in doing that."

"I have an old motorcycle that I don't ride anymore. You can have it if you'd like, but you'll have to get it started."

"How much do you want for it?"

"I don't want anything for it. You can have it."

"Give me your address and I'll take a look at it."

The following week I called Sean and told him I was on my way up there to take a look at the motorcycle. I stopped at a gas station not far from his house and filled up. I called him from there.

"Hello."

"I'm just up the street from your place. I'll be there in ten minutes."

"Okay, I'll be outside."

"I'll see you when I get there."

When I pulled into the parking lot I saw him standing by the bike, parked there with no cover on it.

I got out of the car and said, "This is old, all right. Why don't you have a cover over it? Has it been sitting out here like this all winter?"

"I told you it was old. It's been parked here for the past ten months. I don't want it. The resident manager has been bugging me about getting it off the lot. He said that if I don't remove it he'll have it towed."

"Why didn't you cover it up?"

"I didn't want that old junk any longer, and I didn't want to put any money into it. You can see that it's falling apart."

"Will it start up?"

"I don't know. I haven't touched it since I parked it. Here's the key."

I stuck the key in the ignition. It turned over several times, but it wouldn't start.

"That thing is old. If you don't want it I'm just going to let them take it."

"Well, I don't want to feel as if I came up here for nothing, so I'll take it."

"What are you going to do with it?"

"I don't know yet. Help me put it in the car."

"Are you serious? It's going to be awfully tight in there, isn't it?"

"I need to tie it down good and tight. Do you have some rope?"

"I'll be right back."

I brought the motorcycle back home with me and got a few new parts for it. I got it running and cleaned it up.

After that I responded to one of the ads for a courier. I went downtown, filled out an application, and got the job immediately—sooner than I had expected.

Riding the motorcycle was cheaper than driving my car, and made it easier for me to avoid getting tickets. At first I didn't make much money, only about $85 to $120 a week, but I wasn't really pressed for money at this point. I was more interested in getting to know my way around the city. In the courier business, time is money.

After my third week my earnings began to pick up. I started making around $150 to $220 a week. Then I went to another company and made even more, and from that one to still another. Some weeks I made as much as $560, but of course I had to work longer hours.

I changed employers about four times, each time for higher pay. All of them would cheat you if they could, and they all operated pretty much the same. Switching from one company to another was like going through a revolving door. Everybody in this business knew everybody else, and they were all looking out for their friends and lying to their clients.

Whenever there was a problem with a client and a chance of losing them, the business would change their name or say they had gotten rid of a particular individual. But nothing really changed. They just moved people around.

I wasn't part of the clique. I took the jobs that no one else wanted—the long and late runs—and I worked in all kinds of weather. I didn't care. I rode year round, even when the roads were wet or covered with snow. The longer I worked as a courier, the better I got at doing it. I actually came to like it.

One day I was delivering a package to the law firm of Ropes and Gray, and I got to talking to the receptionist, whom I had gotten to know fairly well. I asked her, "Are you from around this area?"

"No, I'm from Boston."

"I have a friend in Boston who works for Ma Bell, but I've lost contact with her."

"Is that right? I used to work there myself. What's your friend's name?"

"Jackie Davis."

"I'll find her for you. Just give me a few days."

The following week I again had to drop off a package at that office. The receptionist said, "By the way, I have Jackie Davis's number for you."

"You do? I had forgotten all about that."

"Here."

"Thanks."

I called her after I got home.

"Hello."

"Hi Jackie, I just wanted to let you know that I was released and I've been home for over a year."

"I'm very happy for you but, I'm married now and have two kids. If he knew you were home, he would go crazy."

"Don't worry. I'll stay out of the way. You take care."

"You do the same."

After about eight months my motorcycle started giving me problems. Actually, it was falling apart. In spite of having put a lot of time and money into it I decided it was time to let it go. I traded it in for a new and bigger bike, which I paid off in a year.

Some of the other couriers thought I was crazy for putting a new bike on the streets just to do this type of work. One of them said to me, "Why didn't you get a used bike?"

"I didn't want a used bike."

I left it at that, and he didn't bring it up again. I didn't tell him that the bike was paid off, nor did I ask him why he was taking so much time off. I knew he'd been having problems with his bike and needed to take it in for repairs on a number of occasions. It stayed in the shop for long periods of time. I figured that the longer his bike stayed in the shop, the more work I would get.

After dropping off a package in Baltimore one day, I thought about starting my own courier business.

I had been going into the office of Vice President Walter Mondale at least six times a day in connection with my job, and had gotten to know his receptionist pretty well. She was a white woman, attractive, about 5'7". She weighed about 140 pounds and had long, sandy-colored hair. She was very nice.

"You know," I said to her, "I've been thinking about starting my own business."

"Why not, go for it! It's worth a try, and this could be your first account."

"You could get me this account?"

"Yes. All the messenger requests come through me. I'm responsible for all the mail. I've gotten to know you personally, and I know I can depend on you and trust you with our documents. In fact, there have been times when I've called and asked if you were available."

"You have? I didn't know that. I did wonder why they had me coming in here so often. I thought perhaps they were short of help."

She smiled.

"It was because of my asking for you."

"Gee, thank you. Do I need to draw up a contract?"

"Not necessarily. I know you pick up and deliver packages at other businesses and government agencies, and I'm sure some of the folks at those places feel the same way I do. Get some business cards and brochures made up, and go for it."

"I think I will. Give me a week or so to get myself together."

I gave my employer two weeks' notice, and I paid my rent and other bills two months in advance.

I stayed up late every night for about a week, planning for my business and having brochures and business cards made up.

I went to the District Government and filled out the necessary papers to operate a business, and from there I went to the Internal Revenue Service office for a business identification number.

Then I hired an answering service to take my calls and told Mondale's receptionist I was ready.

A week later I picked up another account. The following day I picked up still another and I hired some help. When I received the check from Mondale's office I told his receptionist, "This is my first check. I'm not going to cash it. I'm going to frame it."

"I wish you luck with your new venture, but I would cash it if I were you."

I never did cash that check. In fact, I forgot where I had put it.

That month I made $3,845. I was so excited, for that assured me that I could make it in this business. The second month I made close to $6,000, and each month thereafter the business grew. I picked up additional help as it did.

I eventually discontinued the answering service and hired one of the women who had worked for them to answer my phones. She was very professional and did her job quite well for about seven months. But then I discovered that I was losing a lot of calls, and I started getting complaints. I came back to the office one day with the intention of looking into the source of the problem, and when I walked up to the door I could hear the phones ringing. I opened the door and found her snoring. When she woke up I paid her and said, "You should go home and get some sleep."

She was speechless.

I fired her and immediately found someone else to fill that position.

When Junior was old enough to get his driver's license, I taught him how to drive and bought him a car, for his school was far away and he wanted to continue going to the school he was in and help out with the business every chance he got. When he got home from school in the afternoon, he answered the phones. Then during his last year in school he had classes for only half a day, and by that time the business was growing so fast that I wanted him to help out downtown as well, so I bought him a motorcycle and taught him how to ride. He was a fast learner.

I decided to trade in my bike every other year, and I always paid it off in the first year. It saved me money in the long run to have a bike I could depend on.

TERMINATION OF PAROLE

I had been seeing my parole officer once a month. One day I said to him, "Mr. Green, I've been on parole for two years and I've had no infractions. Can you see about getting me off of parole?"

"I'm afraid that's impossible. Your parole doesn't end until the year 2036."

"The guidelines say that if you've been on parole for two years and have had no infractions, a recommendation can be made for termination of your parole. And if that's denied and you continue to be free of infractions, at three years it can automatically be terminated."

I had seen that when I read the parole guidelines before leaving the penitentiary.

"That's not true. I've been a parole officer for nine years. I think I should know how it works."

"Would you mind looking into it for me?"

"Sure, I can do that."

After I had been home for three years, I again raised the issue of having my parole terminated.

"How are you doing, Mr. Evans? How's business?"

"Everything is okay. I'd again like you to look into termination of my parole."

"Mr. Evans, I thought we talked about that earlier."

"Yes, we did, and you promised to look into it for me. Well, I have to be going. I have some documents to pick up."

"Okay, you take care of yourself, and stay out of trouble."

I thought to myself, Every time I talk to this guy, I smell alcohol on his breath.

I figured him to be an alcoholic from the very first time we met, though he probably didn't know I was aware of it. I was virtually certain he hadn't done a thing to find out about the parole guidelines. He was a nice enough guy, I guess, a redneck, married, with ten young kids. He lived far out in Virginia. He came into the city and put in his eight hours. Then he went home, drank his liquor, and screwed with his wife. That was all his life consisted of, and it was all he ever talked about.

I went to pick up those documents and then decided to go to the library, where I researched the conditions for termination of parole. I composed a petition for termination, on the basis that I'd been on parole for three years with no infractions, and filed it with the parole board.

I couldn't see myself being on parole until 2036.

The following month I got a letter from the parole board stating that my parole had been terminated. That meant I was now a free man and could go anywhere I wanted. There was one thing about my case, however, that still bothered me: having that criminal charge on my record.

QUEST FOR MY FATHER

In 1983, I drove to North Carolina to visit family. I didn't have a chance to see everybody, but I was particularly anxious to see my cousin William.

"Hey William, what's going on?"

"Hey, Kenzell, I heard you were home. How you doing?"

"I'm okay, glad to be home. How you been?"

"I've been under the weather these past few days. What you been doing?"

"I'm working. Tell me, who is this guy that you say is my daddy?"

"I just saw him at the store. If we go over there now, we might catch him."

We got into my car and drove to the store.

"There he is!"

I got out of the car and walked over to him. I didn't feel the slightest bit nervous.

His back was to me. I said, "How you doing?"

He looked at me and said, "I'm okay."

Then he looked at me again.

"Barney! I haven't seen you in a long time. How you been?"

"I'm okay."

"How's your mom?"

"She's fine."

I hadn't seen her recently. I just told him that.

"It's good seeing you again. I have to be getting home. You take care of yourself."

"You do the same."

We parted, and I went back to the car.

"What's wrong with you? Why didn't you talk to him?"

"William, he's not my daddy."

"That is your daddy."

"He's not my damned daddy, and stop saying that."

"I'll leave it alone."

As we were heading back to William's house he said, "That's your half brother right there — his son and I is cool. Pull over. I told him about you."

I pulled over in front of the house and saw the guy sitting there on the porch. We got out of the car, and William introduced us. After talking to him for only a short while, I got up and went back to the car.

Once we had again gotten on the road I said to William, "These people are no kin to me. I don't feel anything for them, and we have nothing in common. I don't know where you got this shit from, but I wish you would stop it. You and that guy may be cool, and that's your business, but it has nothing to do with me."

That was the last time William and I ever discussed it.

I stopped at Steve's house before heading back to D.C. Steve was out working in the yard.

"Hey Kenzell, are you on your way back home already?"

"Yeah, but I wanted to stop and see you and Donna first. I was just over at William's house. He took me to see a guy who he claims is my daddy. I've seen that guy since I was a kid. His name is John Bell. He's no kin to me, but William insists he is."

Steve quickly interrupted me.

"Hell no, John Bell isn't your daddy. William doesn't know what he's talking about. He may have overheard something his mama said, perhaps long ago. She probably knows who your real daddy is, but she won't tell. She and Nora kept a lot of secrets to themselves. You don't look or act at all like Bell. You do look somewhat like a guy that Nora used to run around with, but I don't remember his name. He was in the service. I think he was in the airborne division with Joe. He was a paratrooper. Back then everybody was running around and doing their thing. Pam probably knows about that guy, but she wouldn't tell.

"Bell used to work with Papa. He came to the house quite a bit and would sneak to see Nora. They didn't think anybody had seen them, but I had."

"That's where I know him from. I remember him coming around back in those days. And every time I came down here to visit, somehow, I bumped into him and he would ask me about her. By the way, I didn't let William know that I remembered him."

"Joe was married and in the service, but he and Nora were sneaking around together. Mama didn't like that. She told Nora to leave him alone, claiming that he was married and an Indian, and that Joe and his family were nothing but drunks.

"Later on, Joe got Nora pregnant and she had Jack. Then Joe was transferred overseas.

"In the meantime Nora was running around with that guy that Joe knew from the service. Then Nora got pregnant again. I'm not saying he's your father, but you do look and act like him. I don't know what happened to that guy, but he didn't stay around long. I don't think he even knew she was pregnant. He always said this place was too slow-paced for him. He set out to make some money for himself. He was always talking about doing something or other. It sounds as if his words could have come right out of your mouth. You act just like him. In fact, Donna and I were talking about you earlier today.

"You were born after Joe returned from the service. Joe and his wife had a daughter together. She and you are around the same age.

"There was talk of Joe leaving his wife for Nora, but he didn't want you, so Mama took you and raised you along with us. That's why you have the same name we do."

"I'm sorry Steve, but I got to cut you off. I got to get on the road so I can beat the traffic. Tell Donna I said hello. I'll have to see her the next time I'm down here."

"Okay, I'll tell her. You drive safely, and take care of yourself."

As I was driving back, thoughts of "my father" stayed on my mind, more so now than ever before. In fact, I had never really given it any thought until William brought it up. I knew Joe wasn't my father, and this business of John Bell being my father was nonsense. Meeting Bell's son had made me feel rather stupid. I think I would have picked up some vibes from one or both of them if he was my daddy, but that didn't happen.

I remembered John Bell very well. He used to work with Papa. He and a few of their co-workers had come around to visit quite often. They would sit under the apple tree and drink corn liquor. When John thought nobody was looking, he and Nora would sneak around to the opposite side of the house.

I was anxious to get back home and back to work. I loved my work, and I took it seriously. I always looked forward to new challenges, and there was never a dull moment. I worked five days a week, plus Saturday and/or Sunday when the demand for our services called for it.

I was downtown one day, sitting in the park and eating lunch, when a young woman and her son and her friend walked by. The woman turned around and yelled at the boy to get a move on, and then she turned back around and said, "I wish his father would take him." She had said it loud enough for the boy to hear.

That got me to thinking about the identity of my own father, so I got up and drove over to Nora's house, hoping she would be alone and would tell me who my father is. It's been almost two years since I last saw her.

"How you doing?"

"I'm doing okay."

I paused for a moment and then asked her, "Who's my father?"

She looked at me with a half-grin on her face and said, "Why have you been asking William questions about me? He doesn't know who I been with. He wasn't there. If you want to know something about me, ask me to my face."

While she was talking I thought to myself, Boy, what a shock! Someone told her about my conversation with William.

"I wasn't asking about you. I'm asking about my father. Who is he? I'm thirty-five years old. Don't you think I have a right to know?"

"That's not important now. He's never done anything for you."

"That's beside the point. I have a right to know who my father is. Your other kids know who their father is."

"William doesn't know who I've been with."

"That has nothing to do with this. I'm not talking about William."

"I don't know why you listened to what William said anyway. Get out of my face and don't bring this up again. In fact, just get out of my house."

That was the end of that conversation, and I left.

FINDING JOE

$\mathcal{I}$ *was finishing up* some business at the Department of Motor Vehicles, as I was leaving I saw Patrice in one of the lines. I walked over to her and said,

"Hi. I thought that was you over here. How are you doing?"

Eight years had passed.

"Hi. I'm fine, but these MFs are getting on my nerves. I hate coming down here. They claim I have some unpaid tickets, so I can't get my license renewed."

"How is everybody doing?"

"They're okay, except Daddy. He's been sick — and in and out of the hospital — for some time. Mama said he has cancer and isn't getting any better."

"Oh, you haven't been over there to see him?"

"No. I've been busy. Shit, he's not going anywhere. I can see him anytime."

"If he has cancer he might not have much time left to live."

"Well, I'll see him when I get there. Oh shit, I forgot that my ride is waiting for me. I have to go. See you later."

"See you."

A few days later I went over to Nora's house. I knocked on her door, and she opened it and said, "Come on in. Where have you been?"

"I've been around, mostly working. I saw Patrice downtown the other day, and she told me that Joe has been sick and in the hospital. We talked for only a minute or two. So I thought I'd stop by to see you. How have you been doing?"

"I've been doing okay. Your daddy is in the hospital, and he's not doing well at all. I told the others, but they said they don't want to go over there to see him in the condition he's in."

"That man is not my daddy, and he didn't raise me."

"Why do you have to be so difficult?"

"I suggest you not go there. By the way, I ran into one of Joe's drinking buddies, a co-worker of his. He said he's been calling here and you won't let him see or talk to Joe."

"Oh, they don't want anything. They're just being nosy."

"They're Joe's friends, not yours. You shouldn't talk about them like that."

"I'll say what I wish about them."

"Did you tell Joe they've been calling and would like to see him?"

"They're not thinking about him. Even Joe can see that now."

"I guess he can, leave it up to you."

"His doctor said he shouldn't be disturbed. He needs his rest."

"Just stop that nonsense! You can't wait till he's gone, can you? Don't you think he's suffering enough as it is, without your nonsense? I'll see you later."

The following day I went to the hospital to see Joe. When I walked up to the information desk, a nurse overheard me when I called his name out and said,

"He was eating okay for awhile, but then he stopped. He tried to end his life the other night, by disconnecting the monitors from his body. He's lucky they got to him in time to prevent that from happening. We did manage to stabilize him, but his health has gotten worse since then."

"What is his room number?"

"It's upstairs in room 246A."

"Thanks."

I took the elevator to the second floor and walked down the hall to Joe's room. When I went in he was lying in bed and staring at the ceiling.

"Hey, how are you doing?"

He turned his head, looked at me, and said,

"Hi. I'm just barely hanging on."

I could see that he had lost a lot of weight. He looked like a skeleton.

"I heard you've been sick."

"I've been sick for quite awhile now. If I had a chance to do it all over again, I would never take a drink."

"Why did you disconnect the monitors, and why haven't you been eating? As long as the heart beats, there's hope. This is the time to be strong, to keep your spirits up, and remember that prayer can work wonders."

At that point tears began rolling down the side of his face. I became silent for a moment. Then I asked,

"Has anybody been over here to see you?"

"Nobody, only your mother has been over here."

"I ran into one of the guys you used to work with, one of your drinking buddies. I don't recall his name, but he asked about you and wants to see you. He said the other guys do too."

"They do?"

"There may be others who feel the same way. Why isn't this television on? Doesn't it work?"

"Nora said I don't need it on."

"Do you want it on?"

"Yes, that would help."

"Okay, I'll take care of it."

I used the phone in Joe's room to place a call to the nurses' station.

"I'd like to have the television turned on in this room."

"Sir, I'll call downstairs and have somebody come up and take care of that for you."

"I appreciate it."

About ten minutes later a woman walked into the room and asked, "Did someone call about having the television turned on?"

"Yes, I did."

"That will cost two dollars a day."

"Ma'am, here's $30. Just turn it on and leave it on."

"This will be enough for 15 days."

"I'll be back before that runs out."

"Thank you," said Joe.

"Think nothing of it," I replied. "Well, I've got to be going. My pager is going off. I'll stop by and see you later."

"Thanks again."

"See what I mean? You're beginning to sound better already."

The following week I got a phone call from Kim.

"I don't know if anybody told you, but Joe passed away. His funeral is …. "

"Thanks, but I won't be going."

"I'm going to go even though Joe didn't treat me the way a father should, he was the only man in my life when we were coming up."

"I understand. I have some things to do, and then I have to get ready for work. You take care."

"All right, I'll talk with you later."

NEW BEGINNINGS

Within five years, a black female entrepreneur client introduced me to the D.C. media arena, and then to the big leagues. I hired more help, since I had to be on call 24 hours a day to accommodate the schedule of people I was asked to drive around. Soon thereafter, I met Dr. Lawrence Jones, the Dean of Howard University and he introduced me to some of his friends.

In the summer of 2003, while I was taking a much-needed vacation, I met Karen Smith. She was vacationing too. She was a nice-looking woman, about 5'7" and 140 pounds. She had a nice body for the bikini she was wearing. When I laid eyes on her she was sipping on a daiquiri and looking sexy. I just had to go after her.

After dating Karen for more than two years, I could tell that she had a lot of the qualities that I liked and wanted in a woman. We got married a short time later. My friend Dr. Lawrence Jones officiated at the ceremony.

Karen and I drove down to our retirement home we purchased before we married. On opening the door, I saw that the floors were covered with water. A pipe under the kitchen sink had burst, and there was water coming out. The entire house had flooded.

We called in an environmental company and had them clean up the place and remove the mold. We got rid of a lot of things, because they had been damaged, so I told them to gut it.

Soon afterward I started having head pains. I was going back and forth to the doctor, then to a specialist to discover my blood pressure was very high. I went to see him on a Friday to hear the test results and he said,

"Your kidneys are not gone but very low. I'm going to prescribe some blood pressure pills for you to get it down. I can give you something to bring it down now, but if it comes down too low call me."

Friday and Saturday I was okay, Sunday night I remember going to the bathroom, but I don't know how I ended up on the floor or how long I had been there. I called my wife, "Karen! Karen! Karen!" She came into the bathroom and said,

"What are you doing on the floor?"

"I don't know why I'm on the floor. I came to use the bathroom, and I must have passed out. All of my strength is gone, help me up."

"How long have you been here?"

"I don't know."

She rushed me to the hospital where I was told my blood pressure had dropped very low and I had lost both kidneys. I couldn't believe it. I was put on dialysis three days a week, for three and a half hours each time.

A month later I had a stroke. I lost feeling in my left side and was unable to walk, the hearing in my left ear was gone, and my left eye was immobile. The doctors said I was bleeding in my brain. They scheduled me for surgery on the following morning, but by the time the surgeon arrived the blood had created a new vessel, so there was no need for surgery.

While lying in bed in my hospital room, I was unable to straighten out my body. It was bent over like a bow, with my head in a downward position. I patted myself up and down on the left side and could tell that even though I was unable to move, nothing was broken. I had been given plenty of warnings and had ignored them, so now I needed to take it easy. I wasn't mad or upset. I knew I was going to be all right.

After a couple days I could stand, but I could barely walk. The doctor told me to call the nurse for help whenever I needed to use the bathroom. Nevertheless, I went on my own. It was hard, but I managed. I wanted to use my own strength to get around, and my success at getting to the bathroom on my own encouraged me to do even more, so I gradually added other exercises to my regimen. I was determined to get myself back to normal, though I kept that to myself.

For the following four days I slept every chance I got. I was still extremely tired. The nurses came in frequently to check my blood pressure, draw blood, sticking me, and giving me pills to take.

One day I asked the nurse about this,

"Why are you sticking me?"

"For your diabetes."

"I don't have diabetes. I'm not taking that."

"Your doctor prescribed this for you. I'm only doing my job."

"I understand, but I'm not taking it. You can forget about that."

"You're not taking it?"

"No."

"You have to take it."

"How many times do I have to tell you that I'm not taking it?"

She left and came back with the head nurse.

"Mr. Evans, you can't be giving my nurses a hard time. They're only doing their job. That medicine is what the doctor prescribed for you."

"Sweetheart, I understand, but I didn't come here to be experimented on. You tell *him* to take it, and tell him I said so."

They left and didn't return.

I felt what the doctor had given me caused this to happen to me and I felt there wasn't much I could say because I had flushed the rest of the pills down the toilet before going to the hospital. It stayed on my mind for a long time, and knowing there was nothing I could do about it now but get rid of him.

A few days later a woman from the therapy department came in to see me.

"Mr. Evans, we have you scheduled for therapy tomorrow morning after your dialysis."

"All right."

The next day a young woman came in with a wheelchair.

"Mr. Evans, are you ready?"

"I don't need a wheelchair. I want to use my own strength. I'll walk."

"Are you sure? Wouldn't it be easier to use the wheelchair to get around?"

"I'm okay. Just show me where you want me to go."

"Okay, but I'll take the chair along in case you get tired."

I walked to the therapy center and sat down. There were about 20 people there.

"You're doing great, Mr. Evans. Your drive and determination are unbelievable."

"What's next?"

"You'll have to wait a few minutes. I have to work with someone else right now."

"All right."

Another stroke patient came in, and I asked him about his condition.

"When did you have your stroke?"

"About 18 months ago."

"And that's the best you can do?"

"Man, I'm in no hurry. I'm in the service."

"I see."

I waited ten minutes and started doing another exercise on my own. I was hoping the nurse would come back over and see me, but she didn't. When I finished exercising, I announced that I was going back to my room.

Karen came to see me every day, even when she was tired after a full day at work. A few friends who knew I was in the hospital came to see me as well.

After I'd been in the hospital for about a week and a half, the doctor and Karen came into my room together. The doctor spoke first.

"How are you doing?"

"I'm okay, ready to go home."

"You need to stay here."

"I'm ready to go home."

"Let the hospital take care of all your needs."

"Did you hear what I said?"

Then my wife spoke up.

"Honey, he's the doctor."

"I don't care who he is. They can't do anything else for me, and I don't need to be here. I'm ready to go home."

The next day my wife came and discharged me and on the way home I told her I didn't trust that doctor and wanted to seek another one. She took three weeks off from work to be with me. She was doing everything for me, after the second day I felt helpless. I wanted to do for myself. I started going downstairs at five in the morning and working out until six. She would get up and fix me breakfast and have me at the dialysis center by 6:45 a.m. And come back and pick me up at 10:30 a.m.

She had a therapist come to the house twice a week. He had only one technique that was effective. Everything else I had already been doing on my own. After three visits I said,

"You don't have to come anymore."

I continued exercising on my own, and about two weeks later I decided to turn off the television. I had come to the realization that it was a distraction, one that was prolonging the healing process.

I had been home for about four and a half months and was now walking one mile a day after my dialysis.

Months later after my dialysis was over on Friday morning, I got into my car and drove to North Carolina to assess the work they had done on our retirement home. When I walked in, the first thing I noticed was that the flooring had been replaced. I went through the whole place and inspected it carefully. I was satisfied with their work.

I thought to myself, what am I going to do now? The market is weak. If I sold the house, I would definitely lose money on it.

I sat down on the floor and thought about it. It was a nice brick home, well built, but I was more interested in the land than in the house. I got up, went outside, and walked around the house, pondering what to do.

I decided to keep the house, and I knew it would cost a lot to have someone put it back together.

While I was down there I visited a cousin who was surprised to see me.

"Kenzell, we heard you had been in the hospital, and wasn't doing very well, and here you are down here — you look good. You drove down here alone? Does anybody know you're here?"

"No, and I'm alone. I'm doing fine. I can't jump over the log right now, but I'm okay."

"When did you lose your kidneys?"

"It's been a year now."

"Damn, and you had a stroke too, man, you are blessed."

"Is that what you call it?"

"Well, for someone who has gone through what you have and still look the same, you're blessed man."

"Well, you should have seen me last year."

THE TRANSPLANT

When I got back home Karen said to me, "Junior and I were talking about going in to see if we are a match for you."

"You were huh?"

I didn't say anything else, because I never really worried about it. I just knew I was going to be okay. It was something that happened to me and now I have to deal with it just as I've done in the past. Only this time it's my health. I had no doubt I would get myself back together despite what others may have said or thought about my condition.

I've always felt it was God's way of slowing me down because I received plenty warnings and I disregarded them. I knew HE didn't bring me this far to drop me. HE could have done that when I had the stroke. But instead, he gave me the chance to get up and brush myself off and move on.

At any rate, about a week later Karen said, "Both of us were a match, Junior said he wanted to do the surgery."

I didn't say anything and never spoke a word to him about it, and he never spoke a word to me about it.

My predicament was between God and me. I asked him to fix it, I prayed on it everyday, all day as I've done in the past. HE didn't let me down back then, HE fixed it. In each occurrence HE fixed it. I have faith that HE will do it again.

Less than two weeks I got a call from the hospital telling me to report there in two weeks for surgery, giving me the date and time. I was there, accompanied by my wife. My son was there with his family and we all waited in the waiting area. We still hadn't talked about it. We talked about work, the grandkids, etc., and were told the surgery would take about four hours.

The surgery was a success and Junior went home the next day. The second day I was told I could go but I stayed another day, I wanted to be sure I was okay.

When I came home I called him.

"Are you okay?"

"I'm fine."

"Are you okay?"

"I'm good. Thanks.

"It's okay Dad, I know you would have done the same for me."

"You be sure to get your rest man. Talk with you later."

"I will."

THE REVELATION

About a month later I drove through my old neighborhood looking for somebody I knew who did home improvement work. As I was coming to a stop for a red light, I heard somebody blowing their horn. When I looked to my left, I saw the guy in the car next to mine had a big smile on his face, saying "Kenzell, Kenzell." I rolled my window down so I could see. It was a guy from the neighborhood. His name was Twig. We had gone to school together.

"Kenzell, you got a minute? How about pulling into that gas station lot?"

"I'll follow you."

I followed him, and we got out of our cars.

"I thought that was you back there. When did you come home?"

"I've been home since 1982."

"Kenzell, I didn't know that. What have you been up to?"

"Not a thing. I've been under the weather for some time now. I'm looking for somebody to do some home improvement work for me. Do you know of anyone?"

"I do all kinds of home improvement work. Business is slow right now, so I can go take a look at it. What's your address?"

"The house is down south."

"Oh, what would be the best time for me to call you?"

"Tonight around 7:00 p.m.?"

"I'll give you a call tonight. Right now I have to get back to a job I'm working on."

"All right, I'll talk to you later."

Twig called that night, and we talked about it.

"Twig, after I thought about it, I realized that the house is too far away for you to be running back and forth, so I've decided to do it myself."

"Kenzell, you're in no condition to do that. Let us do it for you."

"I know how to do it, and I'm in no rush."

"Kenzell, I'm behind on paying my mortgage. I need the work. Let me ride down there with you and take a look at it. I'll give you a real good price if I do the job."

"I'm going down there Friday night. If you're not doing anything, you're welcome to ride along. You can take a look at it and then let me know what it would cost. I'll be leaving here a little after midnight, but I won't be coming back until Sunday. If you need to get back right away we'll have to drive down there in separate cars."

"I'll be at your house on Friday night."

He arrived around midnight.

"Twig, you don't have to go man."

"No, I want to see it. And I don't have to get back here for anything special this weekend, so how about if I drive and you ride with me?"

"You don't trust my driving?"

"No man, that's not it. You should be getting your rest."

Twig evidently thought that because of my medical condition I couldn't do a thing. I assured him that that wasn't the case. Nevertheless, I decided to ride along with him.

On the way down, he began to reminisce.

"Kenzell, it's been many years since I last saw you, but I remember that night very well. I stopped by Willie's place, he and some other guys had a white girl in his apartment, and they were talking about raping her. I left because I didn't want any part of it."

"What white girl? What are you talking about?"

"You lived in the same apartment building as Willie, didn't you?"

"Yeah, but this is the first time I've ever heard of a white girl being in his apartment. I never knew that Willie had ever been involved in anything like that."

"I remember going upstairs to your apartment."

"You may have gone to my apartment, but I wasn't there. Back then I worked at night."

"Man I'm sorry. I thought you were there. Maybe it was your wife. I do remember going upstairs."

I felt he had probably told other people this same story back then.

"Thanks for telling me this."

"I can remember your wife dropping you like a hot potato. People were telling her to forget about you, that it would be a long time before you got out."

"Thanks again."

"Don't say I'm the one who told you about it."

"Why, is it a secret?

"Nah."

"Don't worry. I'm not going to mention your name."

He didn't respond to that. To break the silence, I gave him directions for the next leg of our trip.

"Stay on route 85 for a good hour, and then get off at Henderson. I'm going to take a nap. Wake me in an hour."

I didn't take a nap, and instead pondered what Twig had just told me. If that was true, then Willie knew who that girl was, but he told me all along that he had never seen her before, unless it was another girl, or something they were doing. Either way, I had believed him. He had taken me down with him. I suspect there were rumors going around that I had raped some white woman. Now it's been over 40 years and this coward-ass nigger tells me not to mention his name.

Then it dawned on me, after all these years I never thought about it. When I was young and got locked up for the incident that occurred at the church. Willie and I were together, but his name was never mentioned and when I came home this time, he appeared out of nowhere.

My thoughts were interrupted by Twig.

"Hey Kenzell, Henderson is coming up."

"Okay. Are all right?"

"I'm okay."

"We'll be there in two more hours."

"Man that was some rotten shit Willie did. Y'all were friends one time and y'all married two sisters."

"That's water under the bridge now."

"I've seen him several times since he been home, but I stay my distance from him, I'm sure others do to."

"That's water gone down stream."

We never discussed it after that.

As our destination drew near, we stopped and had some breakfast and then proceeded to the house.

"Here it is."

"Damn! Is all of this yours?"

"It suppose to be."

We entered the house.

"Kenzell, we can do this. We can knock this out in a week. We would have to stay down here."

"I'm thinking about doing it myself, I got plenty of time. Besides, I'm thinking about make some changes."

"We still can do the work."

"I said I'm thinking about doing it myself."

"Have you thought about selling it?"

"I have considered that, but I think I'm going to hold onto it."

I never considered our trip down there to be a waste of time — far from it, in fact. What he told me about Willie had lifted a huge burden from my mind. I never told him just *how* important that was to me. I had been in the presence of other people from the neighborhood, and if he knew something, they knew something too, but they never said a word. At least, I found out who my friends are. That might be the reason HE sent me in another direction.

I gave Twig something for his time, but mainly for the information he had rendered. Though, I didn't tell him.

When we got back home, I met with an attorney and informed him of my case and new evidence. I wanted to reopen my case. I furnished him with my transcript and all the other documents pertaining to it.

We got together three or four weeks later.

"Your parole was terminated three years after your release. That kicked you out of the system, which means you can't reopen your case. At this point my only option is to petition the president of the United States for a pardon on your behalf. The problem with that approach is that you'd have to plead guilty, and I doubt that you'd want to do that after all you've been through."

"No, I'm not pleading guilty."

"I would advise you not to seek revenge. At least you know now. Oh, remember, your caseworker gave you a clue too. I would think that that must be a big relief in and of itself."

"It is, after forty years."

"You've come a long way, and I recommend that you just keep on going and never look back."

"Thank you for your time."

"Anytime Evans, You take care."